ISSUES AND PROBLEMS IN THE SOCIOLOGY OF JAMMU AND KASHMIR

EDITORS

DR. MUDASIR A. LONE
SUDESH KUMAR

i

ISSUES AND PROBLEMS IN THE SOCIOLOGY OF JAMMU AND
KASHMIR

ISBN-13: 978-1499155044
ISBN-10: 1499155042

Published By:

CREATESPACE INDEPENDENT PUBLISHING PLATFORM

TO

GRANDFA

HAJI ABDUL AZIZ LONE

Acknowledgements

The editors are very thankful to the contributors who readily offered their worked out research studies and papers for this book to make it a multidimensional edited volume for research and reference. We thank Mr. Aijaz Bhat from the designing and Createspace Publishers who helped us in bringing this book out. The formatting of this book is inspired by the edited volume of Morris Rosenberg and Ralph H. Turner "Social Psychology: Sociological Perspectives".

EDITORS

ISSUES AND PROBLEMS IN THE SOCIOLOGY OF JAMMU AND KASHMIR

ISSUES AND PROBLEMS IN THE SOCIOLOGY OF JAMMU AND KASHMIR

CONTRIBUTORS

1. **DR MUDASIR AHMAD LONE**

   EDITOR, REVIEWER &
   ADVISORY MEMBER IJMER

2. **SONIKA SEN**

   DOCTORAL SCHOLAR;
   DEPARTMENT OF
   SOCIOLOGY
   UNIVERSITY OF JAMMU

3. **KANDEEL KASHYAP**

   PHD SCHOLAR; DEPARTMENT
   OF SOCIOLOGY
   GURU NANAK DEV
   UNIVERSITY;
   AMRITSAR INDIA

4. **SHABEER AHMAD BHAT**

   DOCTORAL SCHOLAR;
   DEPARTMENT OF
   SOCIOLOGY,
   UNIVERSITY OF KASHMIR

5. **GOWHER AHMAD SHALLA**

   PHD SCHOLAR; DEPARTMENT
   OF SOCIOLOGYGURU NANAK
   DEV UNIVERSITY;
   AMRITSAR INDIA

6. **MUSHTAQ AHMAD DAR**

   LECTURER HISTORY

7. **SHAHID SHAFI ITOO**

   LECTURER ENVIRONMENTAL
   SCIENCE; SECONDARY
   SCHOOL EDUCATION
   DEPARTMENT
   GOVERNMENT OF JAMMU
   AND KASHMIR

8. **MS. RUCHI**

   PHD SCHOLAR; DEPARTMENT
   OF SOCIOLOGY, UNIVERSITY
   OF JAMMU; J & K INDIA

9. **TSERING JOLDEN**

PHD SCHOLAR; DEPARTMENT
OF SOCIOLOGY
UNIVERSITY OF JAMMU; J & K
INDIA

10. **RAMEEZ AHMAD MIR**

LECTURER HISTORY

11. **RAVI KUMAR**

PHD SCHOLAR; DEPARTMENT
OF SOCIOLOGY
UNIVERSITY OF JAMMU
180006; J & K INDIA

12. **SUDESH KUMAR**

DOCTORAL SCHOLAR;
DEPARTMENT OF
SOCIOLOGY GURU NANAK
DEV UNIVERSITY; AMRITSAR
INDIA

13. **GOUSIA YASIN**

RESEARCH SCHOLAR;
DEPARTMENT OF
SOCIOLOGY
UNIVERSITY OF KASHMIR

14. **UMAR MANZOOR MIR**

M.PHIL HISTORY; A.P.S
UNIVERSITY REWA; M.P INDIA

Table of Contents

Preface

The book provides an insight into if not all but at least into the burning issues and themes of sociological research in the society of Jammu and Kashmir. It offers a broad spectrum of topics so that scholars from the field of sociology and anthropology may take some help to devise new topics and undertake appropriate research techniques while dealing with different social settings throughout the state of Jammu and Kashmir. The book as we hope will serve as a guide to scholars particularly in sociology for further research by giving them an idea about the most suited research tool and design for their studies.

CHAPTER-I GENDER AND SOCIETY is an attempt to work out the impact of a particular social set up on various socio-economic aspects and issues pertaining to gender like socio-economic status, women rights, education and literacy. The study is based exclusively on Pakhtoon women whereby focusing mainly on the present socio-cultural status, a comparative analysis has been sought out among the Pakhtoon women of Afghanistan, Pakistan and Kashmir valley in India.

CHAPTER-II SMALL HANDS, BIG RESPONSIBILITIES attempts to study the problem of girl child labour under the age of 18 years in paid domestic services in Jammu. The chapter probes into the impact of poverty, schooling problems, uneducated parents and employment of girl in domestic labour.

CHAPTER-III OBC'S POLITICAL PARTICIPATION AND RESERVATION RIGHTS IN JAMMU AND KASHMIR In Jammu and Kashmir (J &K)OBC nomenclature has been changed to OSC. Under this category 2 percent quota is given and not 27 percent as in case with other parts of country. Majority of people deprived from their right from last 22 years after the implementation of 27 percent quote for them in the state and central institutions. Mandal Commission report of 1980 quoted OBC population at 52 per cent and provided them 27 per cent reservations in public sector employment and higher education.

CHAPTER-IV THE MENACE OF BEGGING IN THE CITIES OF KASHMIR: A SOCIOLOGICAL ANALYSIS This study provides a sociological foundation for future research on the problem of begging in Kashmiri cities. As begging is emerging as a modern social problem confronting not only to the Kashmir but also the whole world so this chapter is going to understand and analyze different aspects of begging. The central focus is to find the causes of begging and then to identify various consequences.

CHAPTER-V ASPIRATIONS OF EDUCATED GIRLS IN RURAL INDIA: THE CASE OF JAMMU AND KASHMIR Every individual has lot of aspirations like good job, successful business, wealth, power and respect in the family as well as outside, knowledge, freedom etc. and try to find out the ways to get these aspirations full-filled. So is the case with educated women and girls who wish to overcome the age old traditions, restrictions imposed on them by the men folk and they are treated in the society in such a way as they have no identity and no right to dream.

CHAPTER-VI A HISTORICAL STUDY OF CHINAR TREE IN KASHMIR (INDIA): AS THE TREE OF HERITAGE This chapter throws scholarly limelight on the history of Chinar tree (*Platanus orientalis*) in Kashmir. It is called as *"Bune"* in the Kashmiri language, the Chinar tree is an integral part of Kashmiri culture. Almost every village in the valley has a Chinar tree. Having such a splendid history of the Chinar tree in Kashmir, making its presence felt from so many centuries before. It has been praised by many Suffi's and Reshi's of our land. Now chinar is the state tree of Jammu & Kashmir state. So it should be considered as the part of our culture, and the tree of heritage.

CHAPTER- VII UNDERSTANDING THE DRAINAGE PATTERN IN URBAN INDIA: STUDY OF SRINAGAR CITY IN JAMMU AND KASHMIR is an attempt to assess the drainage system and its associated links in these areas so as to get an idea of the whole scenario of the drainage availability and its need in the Srinagar city. Although the work may not expose the Whole picture of drainage system of Srinagar city, however, it may be regarded as the mark of beginning for such studies in the state of Jammu and Kashmir so as to have the knowledge about various socio-ecological problems of this state.

CHAPTER- VIII WOMEN EDUCATION IN INDIA; WITH SPECIAL REFERENCE TO JAMMU AND KASHMIR traces the trajectory of women's education in India while specifically focusing on the state of Jammu and Kashmir. Women constitute almost half of the total human resources (population) of India. Unfortunately, denial of equal socio-economic opportunities and strong traditional bias against women have resulted in low human development indices over the years, as India, like many other developing nations, has lagged behind in upgrading the status of half of its women, in many respects.

CHAPTER-IX A SOCIOLOGICAL STUDY OF SOCIETY IN LADAKH: AN ANTHROPOLOGICAL OVERVIEW The chapter is an attempt to provide a sociological overview to understand the society in Ladakh from an anthropological perspective. It has been conducted within the larger framework of Structural-Functional approach. It attempts to understand the structure of both family and marriage among the Buddhists and the functions these structures plays in this society.

CHAPTER-X INVESTIGATING CULTURE AND TRADITION IN ARCHITECTURE: A SOCIO HISTORICAL STUDY OF HINDU TEMPLES OF KASHMIR VALLEY IN J & K INDIA bring into scholarly limelight the traditional and historical aspects of Hindu temples of the valley of Kashmir in the state of Jammu and Kashmir of India. The main focus here is to analyze the tradition of temples from time to time through the history of the valley through a socio-historical perspective. The findings were collected from a civilizational angle to unfold the archeological situations the Hindu temples have witnessed through the political history from the then princely state of Jammu and Kashmir till date.

CHAPTER- XI DISABLED CHILDREN: CONCEPT, PROBLEMS AND CHALLENGES; WITH SPECIAL REFERENCE TO JAMMU AND KASHMIR Children and young people with disabilities continue to be one of the most disadvantaged groups in all our societies. In fact, disability and its conceptualization are cultural and social constructs. Disabled, thus, as a category are socially excluded and continue to be marginalized in our societies. The study is an attempt to understand in its micro context the lives of the children suffering from various disabilities which have invariably brought into focus the care that they receive within their homes as well as in the institutions. The study has also brought into light the problems associated with parenting children with special needs. The interactionist approach to the study of disability has been made use of.

CHAPTER- XII SOCIOLOGICAL IMPLICATIONS OF DEVELOPMENT PROJECTS IN INDIA: WITH A CASE STUDY OF DUL AND HASTI PROJECT IN KISHTWAR, JAMMU AND KASHMIR INDIA The chapter seeks to reveal the various socio-economic implications of the power developmental projects both positive and negative. The social issues arising out of such projects include forced migration of the local population, employment and labor issues, educational transitions of the student folk besides gender issues. Attempts have been made to interrogate into the processes of social mobility, stratification and differentiation arising due to the transitions towards set back or forwards in the economic system of the areas under and near such developmental projects.

CHAPTER- XIII SCIENCE EDUCATION AMONG KASHMIRI FEMALES: a STUDY OF DISTRICT ANANTNAG is based on fieldwork conducted in district Anantnag of Jammu and Kashmir in India. It aims to investigate the present status of female science education in the district. It also aims at studying the effect of traditionalism, economic conditions and family attitude towards science education. Main focus of this deliberation is to analyze the interest of Kashmiri females towards science education and to find the percentage of Kashmiri women opting for science education.

CHAPTER- XIV THE HISTORY OF CULTURE AND TRADITION: KASHMIRI PANDITS IN JAMMU AND KASHMIR reveals the historical background of the culture and tradition of the Kashmiri Pandits. The ritual culture of the people of Kashmir grew from its *Burzahom* past and is, therefore, formed of several sediments; the basic sediments have their origin in the ritual structure of Burzahom people and the people of Kashmir who lived through the Nilmat period. Some of the ritualistic practices of the Kashmiri people have been inherited from the Aryans travelled to the state of Kashmir and settled there with the original inhabitants of Kashmir.

CHAPTER-I

GENDER AND SOCIETY

PAKHTOON WOMEN OF AFGHANISTAN, PAKISTAN AND KASHMIR VALLEY; A COMPARISON

DR. MUDASIR AHMAD LONE

Pakhtoon Women of Kashmir Valley: Outline of the Status

The lives of Pakhtoon women vary from those who reside in conservative rural areas, such as the tribal belt, to those found in relatively freer urban centers. Though many Pakhtoon women remain tribal and illiterate, others have become educated and gainfully employed. In Afghanistan the ravages of the Soviet occupation and the Afghan wars, leading to the rise and fall of the Taliban, caused considerable hardship amongst Pakhtoon women as many of their rights had been curtailed, in favor of a rigid interpretation of Islamic law.

The difficult lives of Pakhtoon female refugees gained considerable notoriety with the iconic image of the so-called "Afghan Girl" (Sharbat Gula) depicted on the June 1985 cover of *National Geographic magazine*. In addition in the rest of Asia, particularly in the rural settings, the male-dominated code of *Pashtunwali* often constrains women and forces them into designated traditional roles that separate the genders. The pace of change and reform for women previously has been slow as a result of the conservative social set up of Pakhtoon societies but modernization and education has to a considerable extent lead to the empowerment of Pakhtoon women (Benedicte, 1992).

Modern social reform for Pakhtoon women began in the 20th century. During the early 20th century, Queen Soraya Tarzi of Afghanistan had been an early feminist leader whose advocacy of social reforms for women proved so radical that it led to the fall of her and her husband King Amanullah's dynasty. Even during the tumultuous Soviet occupation of Afghanistan, civil rights remained an important issue as feminist leader Meena Keshwar Kamal campaigned for women's rights and founded the Revolutionary Women of Afghanistan (RAWA) in the 1980s.

Today, Pakhtoon women vary from the traditional housewives who live in seclusion to urban workers, some of whom seek or have attained parity with men. Due to numerous social hurdles, the literacy rate for Pakhtoon women remains considerably lower than that of males. Abuse of women has been widespread, yet women's rights organizations, which find themselves struggling with conservative religious groups as well as government officials, have been actively challenging the practices. Benedicte writes "a powerful ethic of forbearance severely limits traditional Pashtun women's ability to mitigate the suffering they acknowledge in their lives" (ibid).

As one can see among Pakhtoon women today, there are two main divisions or sections of them, the age group of up to 30 which includes the girl population in their teens and young ladies and the second comprises the age group of 40 and above. There is a marked difference in the ideology of these two groups due to the impact of assimilation viz-a-viz modernization on the former group and of the traditionality and an ideological attachment with the tradition on the latter one. The responses/views of these two groups regarding some developmental issues related to assimilation are indicated in table 1 below:

Women Group	Social Issue	View/Response
Up to 30	Women education	Strongly agree
	Jobs by women	Agree
	Age at marriage.	20-25
	Women as head of family	Agree
	Cultural expression of women	Agree
	Women in singing & other such areas	Agree
40 & above	Women education	Agree
	Jobs by women	Partially agree
	Age at marriage	18-20
	Women as head of family	Don't agree
	Cultural expression of women	Don't agree
	Women in singing & other such areas	Don't agree

Table 1 : There is a clear impact of the assimilation on the ideology of the Pakhtoon women as it is on the men folk since the last two decades in particular.

Source: Field based data.

Issues and Problems in the Sociology of Jammu & Kashmir

Today Pakhtoon women are on the front not only in singing, sports and fashion but in military and politics throughout Asia. There is a new trend which is taken as a matter of pride that is to send girls for professional courses like Computer Science and Management. *Noreen*, a BCA student from Anantnag district of Kashmir wants to do masters in Computer Science and go for an academic job. The main obstacles to women empowerment, the ideological and traditional restrictions are gone and now socio-economic development is the variable on which the development of Pakhtoon women depends. It is a general observation that Pakhtoons nowadays do not wait to invest on the education and all round development of their girls when they have the resources for it.

As found during the present study about 80 percent Pakhtoon women favor the present trend of their development and empowerment particularly receiving good education, doing jobs and giving away of the strict traditions like women should remain in the four wall, women cannot do any job and the like. There may be a little or more disfavor to these modern values regarding the women status by the dominant male population in their patriarchal society but the fact is that Pakhtoon women surely want to come out of the veil, receive sound education and skill, work as their males do and want to express themselves, their talent and skill to the people of the valley and to the people of the world.

Social restrictions and the present status

Free mixing between genders only takes places within families. In professional situations such as at businesses or universities, males and females may be co-workers, but are nevertheless cautious to maintain each other's honor. Foreign females must learn to read the rules and live by them. If a man speaks to you directly in a social context, he is dishonoring you. If someone speaks to you on the street, that is equally inappropriate. Pakhtoons avoid looking men in the eyes, and keep eyes lowered while walking down the street to maintain reputation.

Women must always dress properly to avoid unwanted attention. They should wear loose fitting pants under their skirts and be sure the definition of legs is undistinguishable. It is also strongly advisable to wear a headscarf in public. On the other hand foreign men should note that it is inappropriate to initiate social conversation with a woman, and one should not ask a male about his wife or female relatives. Men and women should never be alone in the same room. If this happens one should ensure a door is left open. Men and women should never touch one another under any circumstances (Ali, 1995).

Issues and Problems in the Sociology of Jammu & Kashmir

The changes in the ideology have had more impacts on issues like this one as shown by the close investigation of the gender gap among Pakhtoons. As observed on occasions of marriage, fairs and festive gatherings, the young people seem to mix freely with guests irrespective of being from within or outside their ethnicity. Though there may be separate tents for males and females to celebrate the *mehandirat,* there are not as strict gender demarcations nowadays as they used to be even only thirty years ago.

Modernization and the contemporary education have changed not only the social but the psychological nature of the traditional restrictions of the Pakhtoon society in general and of Pakhtoons of Anantnag in general. The cultural restrictions are fading away or perhaps have already gone at least among the younger generations since last 30 years in Anantnag.

The Pakhtoons migrated into the valley with an estimated literacy of below 10 % for males and below 1 % for females. The enrollment in Afghanistan in 1926 was 21 % with the literacy rate gradually increasing up to 18.7 % for males and 2.8 % for females by 1973-74 as per the United States Agency for International Development and Government of Afghanistan, *National Demographic and Family Guidance Survey of the Settled Population of Afghanistan* I, Kabul, 1975.

Their literacy level has been improving gradually touching an average of 56.33 % with 32.16 % for males and 24.16 % for females in 2011 (As per the research data).

Sex	Literacy at various levels of Education %						Average
	Middle	10th	10+2	Grad.	P.G	M. Phil /Ph. D	All levels
♂	70	65	30	20	7	1	32.16%
♀	65	60	10	7	3	0	24.16%
Average whole literacy							56.33%

Table 2: Literacy of Pakhtoons at various educational levels.

In Pakistan the adult literacy rate for female was 71 percent in the year 2001 and youth literacy rate for females was 57 percent for the same period, the average year of schooling was 2.5 in 2000, which shows a little tendency towards investment in education to females (Kausar).

Division of Labor in Family

Previously the strict observance of purdah resulted in a marked division of labor between the sexes. Today Pakhtoon women of the valley not only participate actively in agriculture but also are doing jobs. However, mainly the division of labor operates on the same lines as among Kashmiris where women are preferred for doing domestic work and looking after the family.

Child marriages are un-common. Polygamy is practiced on a limited scale. A Pakhtoon takes a second wife only when the first one is issueless or differences between the husband and wife assume proportions beyond compromise. Divorces are not common as the Pakhtoons abhor the very idea of a *Talaq* or divorce. The word *Zantalaq* (one who has divorced his wife) is considered an abuse and against the Pakhtoons' sense of honor (ibid).

As one can see among Pakhtoon women in the valley today, there are two main divisions or sections of them, the age group of up to 30 which includes the girl population in their teens and young ladies and the second comprises the age group of 40 and above. There is a marked difference in the ideology of these two groups due to the impact of assimilation viz-a-viz modernization on the former group and of the traditionality and an ideological attachment with the tradition on the latter one.

As found during the present study about 80 percent Pakhtoon women favor the present trend of their development and empowerment particularly receiving good education, doing jobs and giving away of the strict traditions like *purdah*, sexual division of labor, women should remain in the four wall, women cannot do any job and the like. There may be a little or more disfavor to these modern values regarding the women status by the dominant male population in their patriarchal society but the fact is that Pakhtoon women surely want to come out of the veil, receive sound education and skill, work as their males do and want to express them, their talent and skill to the people of the valley and to the people of the world.

Pak and Afghan Pakhtoon Women

The role and the situation for women in a traditional, patriarchal society of Pakistan encompass a great bearing. Society has already defined their roles. Discrimination against female child starts from her conception, and continues throughout her life. What happens to her, when she becomes an adult, is subjected to all sorts of exploitation ranging from mental and physical torture to sexual abuse. In patriarchal society as in Pakistan, family is the basic unit which sets the norms for males and females. Within this system, fathers and husbands are recognized as the guardian of women and the decision making power are vested in male hands. The right of inheriting property is passed in the hands of husbands and sons. The kinship system leads to strong preference for son and discrimination against daughters. Male members are the central in lineage. As an adult she becomes extraneous to her family of birth. She lives in her father's home only until it is time for her to marry. It is highly unusual for an adult woman to live with her parental family. "When she got married, her productivity and services are shifted to the husband's family whatever her parents need may be" (Gupta and Shuzhuo, 1999). Parents of young daughters are reminded of their obligation to marry of their daughters. Their appropriate place is in their husband's home as a wife in another family, and after marriage when she joins her husband's family; she has to face difficult circumstances, especially if the husband is residing with his parents.

The expenses of a daughter's marriage are much higher than a son's marriage because large dowries are paid to the groom's family and it is viewed as a loss to the family. So the birth of a daughter is considered less desirable phenomena. The fundamental rights of women are violated in homes and within communities; even the right to take decisions concerning their own lives is not given. Marriage against choice is a deep rooted social problem which is the violation of an individual's basic right. The norms work in a manner that divorce makes the woman a social outcast, by lowering her self esteem. In economically disadvantaged families, the situation of women is worse. Society has imposed the stereo types of gender roles and expectations with the result that it has become unfeasible for women to break out of the vicious circle, in which she has been confined by norms (Ibraz, 1993). In some communities restriction on women are much more stringent which allows greater exploitation and discrimination (Mohanti, 1997). The bottom line of the problem is that she is caught in a situation which she cannot change, that is predetermined and predestined.

Research has proved that education is a sufficient factor to enable women to challenge gender relations, but much is required to change the norms and the critical attitude of society (Jeffery and Basu, 1996; Mason, 1993). Literacy rate has improved in Pakistan in terms of enrollment rate, but there are many structural constraints on women's education and their work choices in terms of occupational rigidities and women's own perceptions and aspirations for adult life. There are clear indications that education and employment decisions of women taken by their parents channel them towards marriageablity. The organization of marriage has gotten much importance due to the lack of women's control over income and property. The emphasis on marriage is due to its value for women in the context of norms of feminity (Eapen, 2002).

Pashtunwali Code and Pakhtoon Women's Legislative Authority

Embedded in the legal history of Afghanistan are the tribal codes of the Pashtun or Afghan tribes, which came together under Ahmed Shah Durrani in 1747 as the confederacy that eventually shaped the modern-day state of Afghanistan. These tribal law codes are called Pashtunwali, and they are widely practiced as a component of customary law, especially in rural Pashtun majority areas. Pashtuns make up the largest ethnic group in Afghanistan. The role of women in Pashtunwali is little studied and even less understood. Much has been written about the oppression of women in Afghanistan, and it is often attributed to Pashtun tribal practices, such as male elders having say over marriages of young women; high bride prices, *walwar*, given to the father of the bride and suggesting the sale of women into marriages; honor killings of women for sexual misconduct (Kakar, 2003).

Among the large Pashtun landowner (*zamindar*) class and among the city-dwelling Pashtuns, the seclusion of women is prevalent and the *chaderi* or *boghra* are worn when the woman leaves the confines of her household compound. Women are constrained by the Pashtunwali code in so many ways that it is difficult to understand why they participate in this system, or why, when women's rights reforms are discussed, they resist them, even those associated with health care and education. Even though there are at present few traditional practices of Pashtunwali that were able to withstand the influence of pervading religio-political ideologies, due to war, drought, and displacement, it is critical for the reconstruction of Afghanistan to understand the "ideal" Pashtunwali in the minds of Pashtun men and women, who may no longer be living in their Pashtun majority communities but yearn to return to a peaceful and "ideal" past (ibid).

While much of the legal process of customary law seems to be in the control of men, there are layers of legislative authority in Afghan rural society that function within specifically gendered networks and others that bridge those gender segregated networks. Pashtunwali is a tribal code, as mentioned above. "If law is a system of enforceable rules governing social relations and legislated by a political system, it might seem obvious that law is connected to ideology," (Christine, 2001)

Women Role and Status in Pakhtoon Society

The study on Pakhtoon women in Peshawar indicates that the women role and status is determined in Pakhtoon society by the male. Her general role is only home management; Cleaning, Washing, Cooking, Budget Making, Agriculture Activities (Livestock & Poultry etc), Sewing and Embroidery making, Socialization of Children, Participation in Ceremonial activities and female oriented Job/ Service. Her contribution in decision making includes; Socialization & Education, Home Management, Health Care, Family Planning, Budget Making, Time table of Work and Game / Play, Salary / Income Keeping and Spending, Participation in Ceremonial Activities, Sharing / Suggestion in Every matter. Her economic role includes; Job / Service, Selling daily used commodities, Live Stock / Milk Products, Poultry Products and Netting, Sewing and Embroidery making and selling. Her social role consists upon; Participation in Marriage ceremonies, Participation in Death Ceremonies, Participation in traditional and all types of ceremonies. Problems faced by women in their productive role-play; Women are less advantaged, lack of mobility, Limited education, no access to resources, invisible partners of development, low health, low levels of nutrition, high rates of mortality, male dominancy and patriarchy. To improve the role and status of Pakhtoon women it was recommended that women education should be improved and they should be given equal participation in developmental activities of the society (Alam, 2012).

Major Schools of Thought on Women Studies

In Pakistan, the legal status of women is drawn from their religious status. Islam enjoins equal status of women and allows female inheritance. Islam also allows female consent for marriage and permitted remarriage by widows and divorces (Rahman, 1987).

Islam encourages education of women so they can teach their modesty by properly covering their bodies (Iqbal, 1988). Although the Quran Sunnah and our history have shown that women can be equal to men provided women should be treated on a pedestal equal to men. From the inception of birth she was given to understand that her most important and fundamental qualities were her dependence and helplessness. She was only prepared for her role of marriage and subjugation to the will of man. This was regarded as the only successful career. She looked upon man as the only means for her subsistence and in majority of cases man became the only breadwinner of the family and hence flattered that woman could not survive without him.

The error of our social system gave man dominating position and created false division between the two sexes, as a social scientist writes: "Man is intended for the work, women for the home, mans strength is in the head, women is in the heart, man's functions is to protect, women to sooth and comfort men must work and women must weep". On the question of women's position in Pakistani society, there are two major opposing and conflicting schools of thought. The religious fundamentalists represent one school, the other by the modernists. According to the fundamentalists, there is a discrete division between men and women. God has entrusted both with unequal and differentiated responsibilities. Man is active and is a provider and an organizer of life in general, while woman is passive and is a caretaker of home and children. Acquisition of knowledge and education is derivable for both men and women; however, their nature and content are to be different from each other. According to the perception of a well known Islamic scholar, Abul Ala Maududi, "The right sort of education for women is that which prepares her to become a good house keeper" (Maududi, 1979, p. 213). As a result of this difference, women are incapable of shouldering the heavy responsibilities of life (Asghar, 1992).

Women of the NWFP

In order to comprehend and appreciate the woman's situation in the predominantly Pakhtoon society of the North-West Frontier Province (KPK) of Pakistan, it is important to understand some of the attribute of Pakhtoon culture. The origin of the Pathan's who are also known as the Pushtuns or Pakhtoons, goes back many centuries (Caroe, 1958). Quaddus (1987) described the Pathan as "a strange warrior race of romantics. Pakhtoon are aggressive, colorfully attired, hospitable and considerable, fierce in enmity, kind in friendship, punctilious over religion yet fond of pleasure".

Tribal customs and traditions form an inseparable part of the Pathan culture. The present day Pathans have undergone many changes as a result of modern influences, but their centuries old traditions and customs have not changed considerably. The Pathan's life is governed by his Pukhtunwali or Pashtunwali, which is an unwritten code of honor. Ahmed (1976, p.75) describes Pashtunwali as a value orientation, which emphasizes "male autonomy, self-expression and aggressiveness for honor ("Izzat"). Pashtunwali, or the code of honor, contains values which are dear to pathan and which regulate all facts of his life. Some cardinal features of the pashtunwali tradition are: Melmastia (hospitality), Teaga (truce). Badal (revenge), Jirga (Deputation) Tarburwali (agnatic rivalry) Nang (honour), and Nanwati (forgiveness) (Caroe, 1958, Taper, 1983, Quddus 1987).

Issues and Problems in the Sociology of Jammu & Kashmir

Pathan women in the rural areas of NWFP are predominately illiterate, tradition-bound and unskilled and they live under highly traditional and conservative social structure, which is marked by its patriarchal male dominance, and religious control. As this society has its own special rules and code of honor women is considered as the symbol of that honor for a Pathan who can reach to an extent in order to save his honor for dies. But under the rules of this society, a woman has her self-respect and identity as a mother, daughter, sister and wife. Beyond these barriers, there is so place for her. As a daughter, as a wife and sister, who serve her male relatives throughout her life but her major power, reflects in her role as a mother. She is the person responsible for the building up of a nation. She can change the destiny of the society because she has the power as a mother to mould the character of the rising generation. (Quddus, 1987).

Aspirations of Pakhtoon Women

It is important to know the aspirations of working women, in the context to understand, what has motivated them to enter the labor market. Aspirations are determined by socio-economic conditions including education and norms adopted by the society. The perception and attitude of women towards job reflect their aspirations. The decision of women to enter the labor market is motivated by the desire to be independent financially because when they work and earn, they become less reliant on their parents and husbands.

Paid-work outside the home makes it possible for women to have aspirations for self-improvement. In developing countries the aspiration of women are simply to work and get economic compensation (in low income strata), without further aspiration of getting a better position by realizing their full potential and minimal opportunities to work (Pangestu and Hendytio, 1997).

Social Restrictions

Women play very little part in the social life. House is the main center of all her activities. Very few women in villages are educated. Even educated girls of cities cannot utilize their abilities. The main reason is that they cannot come out of their houses because of their restriction of purdah. The position of women in Pathan society is not very good in the social life and they do not have even their religious and legal rights. But we must blame only the Pathans for this, as the position of women is more or less the same in other societies? Education can change it to some extent, but on the other hand, very few societies have given such respect as Pathans give to their women. The Pathan society is a traditional and the Pathans are known as brave, warriors, hospitable and good Muslims. This is all due to the lap of that brave and honorable mother in which they grow like other brave and free nations of the world; the Pathans have their own ideology and unique way of life. Their women folk have an important role in the society (Quddus, 1987).

Economic Situation

According to labor force survey in Pakistan only five to ten percent women reported them as working labor force. It does not give us a complete sampling frame of all working women. Usually the nature of women's work is such that it is likely to go unrecorded, because of the informal nature of most of the jobs that women's take up, e.g. stitching at home, embroidery, beauty parlor etc. Secondly the perception is that whatever work goes on within the household is a part of household chores, whether it is an income generating activity or not (Khan 2005). Male members of family are usually reluctant to admit that female members do any work for remuneration. Their economic participation goes unnoticed because they are employed as family labourer or domestic workers without any remuneration.

In the Kashmir valley only 7.2 % of the Pakhtoon women are doing government jobs and are facing the same challenges and restrictions as their counterparts in Afghanistan and Pakistan do. Majority proportion of their population are engaged in needle work (*tilla*), sewing and traditional *Gabba* work.

The economic situation of women exactly portrays the functional theory of gender inequality. It states that: "Female is largely dependent on the male for protection and security". Economically women are projected as very poor and dependent upon men but this is highly a subjective matter. Those who understand the culture and religion, they know it is not the religion which has isolated women from economic activities rather it is the culture which secluded women from earning family life. She is not excluded totally as has been happening in some Asian countries Islam does impose some restriction on women participation in such activities but under certain condition while Pakistan culture is more sever in this regard (Mahbub-ul-Haq Human Development Center, 2000).

References

Abdul, Qudus. (1987). *Pukhtoon Women*, New Peshawar: Awan Publishers.

Ahmad, Aisha and Roger, Boase. 2003. *Pashtun Tales from the Pakistan-Afghan Frontier: From the Pakistan-Afghan Frontier.* Saqi Books.

Ahmed, Akbar S. (1976). *Millennium and Charisma among Pathans: A Critical Essay in Social Anthropology.* London: Routledge & Kegan Paul.

Ahmed, Akbar, S. (1980). *Pukhtun economy and society.* London: Routledge and Kegan Paul.

Ali, Sharifah, Enayat. (1995). *Cultures of the World: Afghanistan.* New York: Marshall Cavendish.

Anwar, Alam. (2000) *Principles of Sociology*, Saif Print's Press: Peshawar Cantt. N.W.F.P. Pakistan.

Anwar, Alam. (2012). "Women Role and Status in Pukhtoon Society (A Case Study of Village Sufaid Dheri, Peshawar)", *International Journal of Learning & Development*, Vol. 2, No. 3.

Asghar, Ali. (1992). *The right of women in Islam*, New Dehli.

Benedicte, Grima. (1992). *Performance of Emotion Among Paxtun Women.* University of Texas Press.

Bourdieu, P. (1966). *The Sentiment of Honour in Kabyle Society.* In J. G. Peristiany (Ed.), *Honour and Shame: The Values of Mediterranean Society.* Chicago: University of Chicago Press.

Caroe, Olaf. (1964). *The Pathans.* London: Macmillan.

Deb, Riechmann. (2006). *Laura Bush Meets Afghan Women*, CBS News, Associated Press.

Debra, Denker. (1985). "Along Afghanistan's War-torn Frontier", *National Geographic.*

Eapen, M. (2001). Women in Informal Sector in Kerala: Need for Reexamination", *Economic and Political Weekly*, June 30.

Gupta, M. D. and L. Shauzhuo. (1999). *Gender Bias in China, the Republic of Korea and India, 1920-1990: Effects of War, Famine and Fertility Decline.* Policy Research Working Paper No. 2140. The World Bank, Washington, D.C.

Hasnain, Nadeem. (1994). *Tribal India*, Delhi: Palaka Prakashan.

Ibraz, T. S. (1993). "The Cultural Context of Women's Productive Invisibility: A Case Study of a Pakistani Village", *The Pakistan Development Review*, 32(1):101-125.

Jeffery, R. and A. M. Basu (ed.). (1996). *Girls Schooling, Women's Autonomy and Fertility Change in South Asia*, New Delhi: Sage.

Kakar, Palwasha. (2003). *Tribal Law of Pashtunwali and Women's Legislative Authority*, Macrothink.

Khan, S. R., S. G. Khattak and S. Kazmi. (2005). *Hazardous Home Based Subcontracted Work: A Study of Multiple Tiered Exploitation*, SDPI, Oxford University Press.

Mahbub-ul-Haq Human Development Center. (2000). *Human Development in South Asia, The Gander Question*, Karachi: Oxford University Press.

Mason, K. O. (1993). *The Impact of Women's Position on Demographic Change during the Course of Development*, In Nora, Federici, et. al. (ed.) *Women's position and demographic change*, Oxford: Clarendon Press.

Mohanti, N. (1997). "Gender Perspective in child labor", *Social Welfare*, 44 (1):10-11.

Muhammad Sharif. (1991). *Women Rights in Islam*, Lahore.

Pangesto, M. and M. K. Hendytio. (1997). *Survey Responses from Women Workers in Indonesia Textile Garment and Foot Wear Industries*, Policy Research Working Paper No. 1755, The World Bank, Washington, D.C.

Tasnim, Kausar. *Labor Market in Pakistan (A Case Study of Bahawalpur District)* Thesis submitted by Department of Economics, The Islamia University of Bahawalpur.

U. S. Bureau of Justice. (1989). *Report of the Gender bias study*, The Supreme Judicial Court, Pakistan Association for women studies Islamabad.

Webliography

BBC World Service. Retrieved 10 October 2006.

Christine, Sypnowich. (2001). "Law and Ideology," in *The Stanford Encyclopedia of Philosophy* (Winter 2001), (ed.). Edward N. Zalta, http://plato.stanford.edu/archives/win2001/entries/law-ideology/

Guardian, 16 January 2006. Retrieved 10 October 2006.

http://www.khyber.org/culture/customs/sociallife.shtml

Making Waves: Interview with RAWA, rawa.org. Retrieved 10 October 2006.

Population by Level of Education and Gender, Pakistan Census, retrieved 10 October 2006.

U.S. State Department's website on Afghanistan: http://www.state.gov/r/pa/ei/bgn/5380.htm

CHAPTER-II

SMALL HANDS, BIG RESPONSIBILITIES

GIRL CHILD LABOR IN DOMESTIC SERVICES

SONIKA SEN

Introduction

Child labour in domestic service is a bitter truth of our society, hidden but known to all. The International Labour Office reports that children work the longest hours and are the worst paid of all labourers (Bequele and Boyden, 1988). Child is the future of a nation and its strength in reserve. The practice of child labour deprives children of their childhood and is harmful to their physical and mental development. This in turn affects a nation's human resource in long term. Girls are found to prefer domestic work as employment worldwide. ILO estimates that more girls under the age of 16 work in domestic service than in any other category of child labour. This paper attempts to study looks into the problem of girl child labour under the age of 18 years of age in paid domestic services in Jammu. The paper looks into various causes which have impact on entry of girls in paid domestic services and working experiences of girl children.

Child labour is different from child work. Child labour can be defined in terms of age and the social situation in which it exists. The age criterion is thus, common in both child labour and child work. The main difference is in the compulsion or lack of it (Bilal, 2010). Child labour is linked to harmful and exploitative activities that threaten the physical, mental and overall growth and development of children. On other hand, the later is associated with activities that are beneficial to growth and development of children and that prepares them to become socially responsible.

The concepts like child, work and labour are encompassed in understanding of child labour. Childhood is generally defined in terms of age. In traditional societies, the accomplishment of certain social rites and traditional obligations are important requirements in defining "adult" and "child" status. In still others, the integration of children into socio-economic life may begin so early that it may be virtually impossible to identify clearly the different life phases. However, in the context of child labour, a working definition of a "child" may be a person below the general limit of fifteen year or in special circumstances fourteen years, set by the Minimum Age Convention, 1973 (No.138).

The International Labour Organisation (ILO) has suggested that the term child labour is best defined as work that deprives children of their childhood, their potential and their dignity and that is harmful to physical and mental development. It refers to work that is mentally, physically, socially or morally dangerous and harmful to children, or work whose schedule interferes with their ability to attend regular school, or work that affects in any manner their ability to focus during school or experience healthy childhood (ILO, 2012).

According to Homer Folks, the chairman of the US National Child Labour Committee, the term 'child labour' is generally used to refer, "any work by children that interfere with their full physical and mental development, the opportunities for a desirable minimum of education and of their needed recreation"(Mishra et.al, 2004).

Gender and child labour

Gender is a crucial determinant of whether a child engages in child labour. Within households, where there are adult men and women, the gendered division of labour generally allocates to women the responsibility for household tasks. Men are considered to be heads of the households, bread-winners, owners and managers of property and active in politics, religion, business and the profession. Women, on the other hand are expected and trained to bear and look after children, to nurse the infirm and old, do all household work, and so on (Bhasin,2000). Girls because of their gender, in almost every patriarchal society are expected to do work at home at cost of their education and leisure time. They do enormous work at home, at the fields and take care for their siblings too. In all societies, boys and girls are assigned different societal roles and experience different perspectives of life as a result of their being male or female, girls are found starting working at an earlier age especially in household chores. Female children work in large numbers and for long hours in and outside the household, but their labour is unacknowledged or underrepresented in formal labour statistics. Parental perception also contributes to the underrating of the labour of the female child.

The issue of gender is now universally regarded as a vital component in addressing child labour. The returns to education may vary with gender. This seems likely to be especially important in third world where men and women participate in different economic activities. Likewise, the returns to activities other than age may also vary across cultures because of discrimination of the sex typing of tasks. Moreover age and gender may interact in important ways. First, girls develop earlier than boys so they may be capable of more sophisticated tasks at certain age. As puberty onsets, boys may develop comparative advantage in more physical activities. Second, the sex typing of tasks may be more important in the types of activities performed by older children. Hence gender difference in household or market work may manifest itself both in the types of activities performed at a given age, and these gender differences may vary with age. The research shows that the largest gender differences are in household production, and these gender differences are increasing in age (Edmons, 2003).

Among girls, domestic work is by far the most common form of informal employment, whether paid or unpaid. But, where it is common, because of the uncertainties, which encircle the children's working situation- which is often confused with alternative upbringing- the practice of taking children into a household for the purpose of using their labour may typically be regarded as socially acceptable, even benign(Sarkar,2010).

By ILO estimates of 2010, 15.5 million children, worldwide, are engaged in paid or unpaid domestic work in the home of a third party or employer and who could be particularly vulnerable to exploitation because of their work is hidden from the public eye, where labour laws can hardly be applied. According to research on children in domestic work, 10.5 million of the estimated 15.5 million children engaged in paid or unpaid work are in child labour either because they are below the minimum age for admission to employment or because their work is regarded as hazardous. Research has also established that 72% of child domestic workers are girls and that 52% of all child domestic workers are engaged in hazardous chores.

In most of the developing countries even today, the female child has a lower status and enjoys fewer childhoods' rights, opportunities and benefits than the male child who has the first call on family and community resources with the female child instigating the process of inequality that the adult woman finds so difficult to overcome. Available evidences show the pride with which a newborn male child is welcomed and the cynicism that greet the baby girl (Anandharaj, 2004).

Paid domestic work is distinctive not in being the worst job of all but in being regarded as something other than employment. The paid work is feminized and informal. The two phenomena are not unrelated. Women's economic activity has, of course, always been characterized by a considerable degree of informality. Unpaid productive labour on farms and in family enterprises, paid work in domestic service in other people's households, street trading and sex work are some of the examples of these more traditional informal activities in which women are disproportionately represented. Informal employment continues to make up a much larger share of women's non-agricultural employment than men's in most developing countries (Hondagneu-Sotelo, 2010).

Causes of girl child labour

Poverty is the most important reason for child labour. Though children are not well paid they still serve as major contributors to family income. The International Labour Organisation (ILO, 2008) and spreading smiles through education Organisation (OSSE) suggests poverty is the greatest single force driving children into the workplace. UNICEF suggests poverty as biggest cause of child labour. Between boys and girls UNICEF finds girls are two times more likely to be out of school and working in a domestic role. Parents with limited resources have to choose whose school costs and fees they can afford when a school is available. Educating girls tends to be a lower priority across the world, including India. Girls are also harassed or bullied at schools, sidelined by prejudice or poor curricula, according to UNICEF. Solely because of their gender, therefore many girls are kept out of school or drop out, then provide child labour (UNICEF, 2001).

Schooling problems also contribute to child labour. No access to school or low quality of education (in case of school accessibility) makes children to seek employment. Parents feel it better to send children to work and supplement family income instead of sending them to schools because schools in rural areas suffer from problems like poor infrastructure, inadequate sanitation, bullying, apathetic teachers etc. A 2012 Wall Street Journal article reports while the enrollment in India's school has dramatically increased in recent years to over 96% of all children in the 6-14 years age group, the infrastructure in schools, aimed in part to reduce child labour, remains poor- over 81,000 schools do not have a blackboard and about 42,000 government schools operate without a building with make shift arrangements during monsoons and inclement weather. Parents who are educated understand the importance of education and schooling. Thus, parents education plays a large role in determining child schooling and employment (Tienda, 1979).

Employing children is an easy option for employers. They find employing children is an as cheap. As adult domestic workers put forward many demands, it becomes easy to handle a child worker. Also with more middle class women moving out to work, the need for domestic labour is also on rise. Employing children at lower wages is an easier option, without having to make any promises and without any tension to meet any demand.

The root causes for domestic child labour are multiple. They can be summarized under push and pull factors. Poverty and its feminization, social exclusion, lack of education, gender and ethnic discrimination, domestic violence, rural-urban migration, loss of parents and diseases ae some of the 'push' factors for child labour worldwide. Increasing social and economic disparities, debt bondages, increasing need for the women of the household to have a 'replacement' at home that will enable more and more of them to enter the labour market and the illusion that domestic service gives the child worker an opportunity for education are some of the 'pull' factors.

Experiences of girl children in paid domestic service

Girl child involved in domestic service are from poor families in rural areas. Poor household income, separation of parents, death of father in family, discrimination for being girl as parents find it better investment to educate boy in family are main reasons for sending them to urban areas for work. Household work is seen as women's work so many employers continue to prefer girls for domestic work. Household work is seen as dirty and inferior job because it involves cleaning of dirt. Because of early training of girls in their homes, they are seen as best fitted for the demands of the work. As there is risk in employing a stronger, most employers prefer to employ young girls as they are more obedient and easy to mould. Majority of girls started working between the ages of 7 to 11. Recruitment is either directly through the employers or through the recommendations of friends and relatives of children's parents. All respondents live with their employers. This gives them chance to enjoy free food and roof but at the same time it means no fixed working hours as they are available for household work at any time. They cannot work at fixed timings and have to adjust according to employer's needs and life-style.

The respondents have to regularly do works ranging from cleaning the house, washing utensils and clothes to looking after children in family. Work period ranges from 5 hours to 10 hours. There reported there are no clear rest hours but they love to watch television and play with children in family which often involves child minding too. Domestic work is among the lowest paid occupations in the world. Being a part of informal economy it does not have any set norm for deciding wages. Majority of girls receive an around Rs. 1500 per month. In remote areas with few opportunities for schooling and poverty, girls are sent in urban areas to work at members of their extended family or some family recommended by person from village with a hope that they will get food, clothes and get a chance to education. "Educational support is probably the biggest contribution a mistress can ever extend to her helper, as it has a long-term impact and can enable the helper to leave paid domestic work and enter into more prestigious job"(Arnado,2003). Many girls working as domestic worker are admitted to schools but they are either not permitted to go to school or allowed to go ones or twice a week. Some of the girls are admitted to government schools in village where they go for taking examination only. Thus, quality education is not provided although girls are enrolled in schools. In many cases girl child is employed for education, clothes and food with no cash remuneration. In few cases where employer provides cash remuneration along with education, the wages are decided between parent and employer and are given to parent direct. However, in such cases more work is demanded.

Although domestic work is a necessity, child labour cannot be justified. There are many difficulties also at work as it is the least regulated of all occupations. Working in the privacy of individual homes, these girls are often invisible to the outside world and thus particularly vulnerable to violence, exploitation and abuse. Some of the respondents reported they are given remaining or wasted food. Many times they are severely beaten and punished by employer. Also, there are incidences of sexual harassment by employers or other household members or guests. Girls because of small age cannot understand the abuse and if they understand they cannot do anything about it because they are living with their employer. Often their position of belonging to servant class creates a divide and they are often not trusted. Girls in domestic work are hidden in private homes, where they are more likely to be abused and less likely to get education.

Child labour prohibition and protection

The Child Labour (Prohibition and Regulation) Act (CLPRA) of 1986 lists hazardous industries in which the employment of children (below 14) is completely banned; in other sectors, it is sought to be 'regulated'. In October 2006, domestic labour and child labour in the hospitality industry were added to hazardous category, banning employment of children. There are no substantive studies to give a true picture of the number of children below 18 in full-time employment in homes. 'Save the Children' has recently estimated that around 50,000 children below 14 work in major cities such as Hyderabad and Kolkata, and at least twice that number in Delhi (Srinivasan, 2010).

The ILO's Committee of Experts on the application of Conventions and Recommendations (CEACR) has been very active in responding to the problem of child domestic labour, given the special attention paid to the matter in the Worst Forms of Child Labour Conventions on forced labour and minimum age, is a crucial source of guidance on the setting of standards to combat child domestic labour. Implementation of the Conventions is facilitated through the provision of substantial technical cooperation, notably through the International Programme on the Elimination of Child Labour (IPEC). The CEACR has repeatedly called upon member States to take effective action to prevent child domestic labour, highlighting the traditional practices of entrusting young children (often distant relatives) to the care of the adults.

At the 100th ILO Annual Conference on June 2011 the government, worker and employer delegates decided to bring domestic workers under the realm of labour standards by adopting an international set of standards with the aim of improving the working conditions of domestic workers worldwide. The international set of standard, that is, the Convention concerning 'decent work' for domestic workers also referred to as the Domestic Workers Convention 2011 (No. 189), provides a clear message that domestic workers like other workers have the right to decent work and living conditions. By these standards, domestic workers should be entitled to the same basic labour rights as those available to other workers such as reasonable hours of work, weekly rest of at least 24 consecutive hours, a limit on the in-kind payments, clear information on terms and conditions of employment as well as respect for fundamental principles and rights at work, including freedom of association and right to collective bargaining. Convention No. 189 and Recommendation No. 201 also specify the need to identify hazardous elements of domestic workers and to prohibit such work for children below the age of 18.

References

- Anandharajakumar P. 2004. *Female Child Labour*, New Delhi: APH Publishing Corporation.

- Anderson, Bridget. 2000. *Doing the Dirty Work?: The Global Politics of Domestic Labour*. London and New York: Zed Books.

- Arnado, Janet M. 2003. "Maternalism in Mistress-Maid Relations: The Philippine Experience". *Journal of International Women's Studies*, 4(3): 154-177.

- Bala, Shashi. 2010. *The Employment and Conditions of Domestic Help in India: Issues and Concerns*. New Delhi: National Labour Institute Research Studies Series No.:088/2010.

- Bequelen, A. & J. Boyden. 1988. "Working Children: Current Trends and Policy Responses". *International Labour Review*, 127 (2): 153-171.

- Bhasin, K. 2000. *Understanding Gender*. New Delhi: Kali for Women.

- Bhat, Bilal A. 2010. "Gender, education and child labour: A sociological perspective". *Educational Research and Reviews Vol 5(6)*: 323-328.

- Edmons, Eric V. 2003. *Child Labour in South Asia*. France: Directorate for Employment, Labour and Social Affairs. pp. 28-29.

- Hondagneu-Sotelo, Pierrette. 2010. "New World Domestic Order" in Jacqueline Goodman (ed.). *Global Perspectives on Gender and Work: Readings and Interpretation*.USA: Rowman & Littlefield Publishers, Inc.

- Lau, Lisa. 2010. 'South Asian Mistresses and Servants: The fault lines between class chasms and individual intimacies', *Pakistan Journal of Women's Studies: Alam-e-Niswan*. Vol. 17, No.1. Pp.33-58, ISSN: 1024-1256.

- Mishra S.N & Shweta M. 2004. *Tiny Hands in the Unorganised Sector*. New Delhi, Shipra Publication.

- Patrinos, H. A. & Siddiqi, F.1995. "Child Labour: Issues, Causes and Interventions". *Human Capital Development and Operation Policy Working Papers*. Washington DC: World Bank.

- Srinivasan, M. 2010. "Domestic child labour: The dirty secret of the rising middle class", *Labour File*, Jan-June. pp 44-45.

- Sarkar, S. 2010. "Girl Child Labour in Domestic Services". *Gender, Poverty and Sustainable Livelihood*. New Delhi, Arise Publishers & Distributors.

- Tienda, M. 1979. "Economic Activity of Children in Peru: Labour Force Behaviour in Rural and Urban Contexts". *Rural Sociology,* 44(2): 370-391.

Internet Sources
- http.www.antislavery.org
- http/ww.hrw.org
- http/www.ghana.gov.in
- http/www.wikipedia.org

CHAPTER-III

OBC'S POLITICAL PARTICIPATION AND RESERVATION RIGHTS IN JAMMU AND KASHMIR

KANDEEL KASHYAP

Introduction

The Central Government of India classifies some of its citizens based on their social condition as *Scheduled Caste (SC)*,*Scheduled Tribe (ST)*, and *Other Backward Class (OBC)*. The OBC list presented by the commission is dynamic (castes and communities can be added or removed) and will change from time to time depending on social, educational and economic factors. For example, the OBCs are entitled to 27 per cent reservations in public sector employment and higher education. In the constitution, OBCs are described as "socially and educationally backward classes", and government is enjoined to ensure their social and educational development. Mandal Commission report of 1980 quoted OBC population at 52 per cent, though National Sample Survey Organization (NSSO) survey of 2006 quoted OBC population at 41 per cent. In a fresh twist to the controversy over the proportion of OBCs in India's population, a government survey released indicated that backward castes formed about 41per cent of the populace.

A survey by the National Sample Survey Organization (NSSO) put the OBC population in the country at 40.94 per cent, the SC population at 19.59 per cent, ST population at 8.63 per cent and the rest at 30.80 per cent. Since the NSSO survey was essentially aimed at measuring the level of consumption expenditure by different households and not estimating the population of OBCs, SCs or STs, the number is not really of great significance statistically.

In fact, a similar survey done in 1999-2000 had put the OBC population at about 35 per cent and it is hardly likely that the proportion has gone up by 6 per cent in just five years the latest survey was done in 2004-05.

The figure of 41 per cent is much lesser than the 52 per cent quoted by the Mandal commission report. The panel had arrived at the figure on the basis of the 1931 caste census by eliminating non-OBC communities from the total population.

According to the survey, 91.4 per cent of STs, 79.8 per cent of SCs and 78.0 per cent of OBCs were in rural areas. Conversely, 8.6 per cent of STs, 20.2 per cent of SCs and 22 per cent of OBCs were in urban areas, while 37.7 per cent of 'others' lived in India's towns and cities.

The booming economic growth seems to be reflecting in the expenditure of urban India, which is spending nearly double the amount on an average compared to the rural areas. The per capita monthly expenditure of people living in urban areas was Rs 1,052.36 a month as against Rs 558.78 of those in rural areas. With minor exceptions, the general level of spending of SCs and STs was lower than OBCs and the others, while that of OBCs in turn was lower than that of the others. According to the NSSO survey, the all India average spending by rural STs was the lowest at Rs 426.19, followed by rural SCs at Rs 474.72, OBCs Rs 556.72 and others Rs 685.31. In urban India, STs spent Rs 857.46, SCs 758.38, OBCs Rs 870.93 and others Rs 1,306.10 in a month on an average.

The survey highlights the fact that in *rural India*, 64.3 per cent of the population continues to be dependent on agriculture as a major source of livelihood, either through self-employment in agriculture (39.4 per cent) or as agricultural labor (24.9 per cent). In this sector, the population dependent on self-employment (agriculture and non-agriculture) was reported to be 49.0 per cent for ST, 36.6 per cent for SC, 60.7 per cent for OBC and 66.4 per cent for others and that dependent on rural (agricultural or non-agricultural) labor was 56.4 per cent for SC, 45.2 per cent for ST, 30.7 per cent for OBC and 21.8 per cent for others. In *urban India*, the proportion of population located in regular wage/salary earning households was almost the same (42.0 per cent to 42.9 per cent) for all social groups except OBCs (34.3 per cent). Dependence on self-employment was more prevalent among OBCs (46.4 per cent) as well as the residual class (45.3 per cent) than the SCs (30.9 per cent) and STs (27.4 per cent).

In economically backward states like Bihar, Rajasthan, Madhya Pradesh and Orissa, SCs and STs were spending between Rs 344 to Rs 527. However, in the educationally advanced state of Kerala, SCs were spending over Rs 750 a month, much higher than the national average.

The Backward Classes Division in the ministry looks after the policy, planning and implementation of programmes relating to social and economic empowerment of OBCs. It also looks after matters relating to two institutions set up for the welfare of OBCs: National Backward Classes Finance and Development Corporation (NBCFDC) and the National Commission for Backward Classes (NCBC).

Backward class people are a collective term, used by the Government of India, for castes which are educationally and socially disadvantaged. They typically include the Other Backward Classes (OBCs). A 1992 decision of the Supreme Court of India resulted in a requirement that 27 per cent of civil service positions be reserved for members of OBCs.

In August 2010 the *Times of India* reported that a most 7 per cent of eligible positions had been filled by OBCs, in spite of the 27 per cent reservation. This difference between proportions of different communities in higher educational institutions is mainly because of difference in primary school enrollment. Political parties in India have attempted to use these communities as vote banks.

Kaka Kalelkar

The First Backward Classes Commission was set up by a presidential order on 29 January 1953 under the chairmanship of Kaka Kalelkar. The commission submitted its report on 30 March 1955. It had prepared a list of 2,399 backward castes or communities for the entire country and of which 837 had been classified as the "most backward".

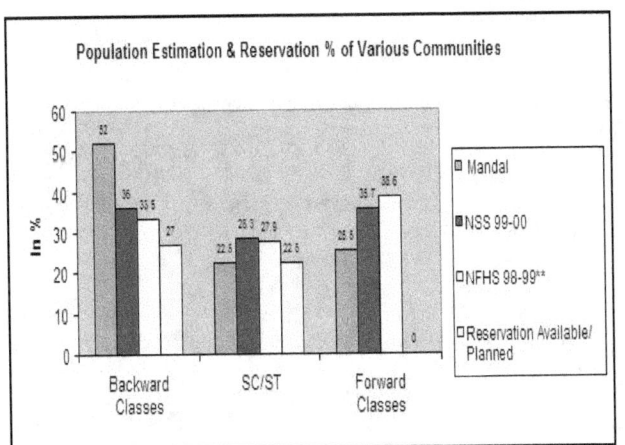

**NFHS Survey estimated only Hindu OBC population. Total OBC population derives by the assuming Muslim OBC population in same proportion as Hindu OBC population.

Issues and Problems in the Sociology of Jammu & Kashmir

Mandal Commission

The decision to set up a second backward class's commission was made official by the president on 1 January 1979. The commission popularly known as the Mandal Commission, its chairman being B. P. Mandal, submitted a report in December 1980 that stated that the population of OBCs, which includes both Hindus and non-Hindus, was around 52 per cent of the total population according to the Mandal Commission.

However, this finding was criticized as based on "fictitious data". The National Sample Survey puts the figure at 32 per cent. There is substantial debate over the exact number of OBCs in India, with census data compromised by partisan politics. It is generally estimated to be sizable, but lower than the figures quoted by either the Mandal Commission or and National Sample Survey.

Under Article 340 of the Indian Constitution, it is obligatory for the government to promote the welfare of the Other 340(1) states, "The president may by order appoint a commission, consisting of such persons as he thinks, fit to investigate the conditions of socially and educationally backward classes within the territory of India and the difficulties under which they labor and to make recommendations as to the steps that should be taken by the union or any state to remove such difficulties and as to improve 'their condition and as to the grants that should be made, and the order appointing such commission shall define the procedure to be followed by the commission."Article 340 states, "A commission so appointed shall investigate the matters referred to them and present to the president a report setting out the facts as found by them and making such recommendations as they think proper."

27 percent of reservation was recommended owing to the legal constraint that the total quantum of reservation should not exceed 50 percent. States which have already introduced reservation for OBC exceeding 27 per cent will not be affected by this recommendation. With this general recommendation the commission proposed the following overall scheme of reservation for OBC:

1. Candidates belonging to OBC recruited on the basis of merit in an open competition should not be adjusted against their reservation quota of 27 per cent.

2. The above reservation should also be made applicable to promotion quota at all levels.
3. Reserved quota remaining unfilled should be carried forward for a period of three years and de-reserved thereafter.
4. Relaxation in the upper age limit for direct recruitment should be extended to the candidates of OBC in the same manner as done in the case of SCsand STs.
5. A roster system for each category of posts should be adopted by the concerned authorities in the same manner as presently done in respect of SC and ST candidates.

Supreme Court conclusions from Ashoka Kumar Thakur vs. Union of India

1. The Constitution (Ninety-Third Amendment) Act, 2005 does not violate the "basic structure" of the Constitution so far as it relates to the state maintained institutions and aided educational institutions. Question whether the Constitution (Ninety-Third Amendment) Act, 2005 would be constitutionally valid or not so far as "private unaided" educational institutions are concerned, is left open to be decided in an appropriate case.
2. The "Creamy layer" principle is one of the parameters to identify backward classes. Therefore, principally, the "Creamy layer" principle cannot be applied to STs and SCs, as SCs and STs are separate classes by themselves.
3. Preferably there should be a review after ten years to take note of the change of circumstances.
4. A graduation (not technical graduation) or professional course deemed to be educationally forward.
5. Principle of exclusion of Creamy layer applicable to OBC's.
6. The Central Government shall examine as to the desirability of fixing a cut off marks in respect of the candidates belonging to the Other Backward Classes (OBCs) to balance reservation with other societal interests and to maintain standards of excellence. This would ensure quality and merit would not suffer. If any seats remain vacant after adopting such norms they shall be filled up by candidates from general categories.
7. So far as determination of backward classes is concerned, a Notification should be issued by the Union of India. This can be done only after exclusion of the creamy layer for which necessary data must be obtained by the Central Government from the State Governments and Union Territories. Such Notification is open to challenge on the ground of wrongful exclusion or inclusion. Norms

must be fixed keeping in view the peculiar features in different States and Union Territories. There has to be proper identification of Other Backward Classes (OBCs). For identifying backward classes, the Commission set up pursuant to the directions of this Court in Indra Sawhney 1 has to work more effectively and not merely decide applications for inclusion or exclusion of castes.

8. The Parliament should fix a deadline by which time free and compulsory education will have reached every child. This must be done within six months, as the right to free and compulsory education is perhaps the most important of all the fundamental rights (Art.21 A). For without education, it becomes extremely difficult to exercise other fundamental rights.

9. If material is shown to the Central Government that the Institution deserves to be included in the Schedule (institutes which are excluded from reservations) of The Central Educational Institutions (Reservation in Admission) Act, 2006 (No. 5 of 2007), the Central Government must take an appropriate decision on the basis of materials placed and on examining the concerned issues as to whether Institution deserves to be included in the Schedule of the said act as provided in Sec 4 of the said act.

Held that the determination of SEBCs is done not solely based on caste and hence, the identification of SEBCs does not violate Article 15(1) of the Constitution. No doubt, there has being done a study on political participation of the OBC's in the village panchayat. It is found that participation in village politics by the OBC's is very low. Awareness and utilization of reservation policy by the OBC 's. Reservation is in the indispensable thing of the Indian society. Reservation in the Indian law is a form of affirmative action, Whereby percentage of seats are reserved in every walk of affirmative action. The recent changes in government policies towards the reservation have made reservation a most talked subject in the Indian society. Government of India reserved seats in the parliament of India, state legislature assemblies, union and state civil servants, public sector units and union State government departments to the deprived section of the society.

According to Khan (1990), hold that reservation means some preference for the disadvantage that may close in an open competition with those who are lucky to have good education, training and upbringing. But Tyagi (1990), holds that reservation area that of social engineering to set the things right and to build just an egalitarian social engineering social order. In government services, special quota is allotted to them. According to Dube (1990), these reservation are not confined to the base at the point of initial recruitment, they were extended the also to promotion for higher position. Both in state legislatures and parliament, they are guaranteed representation.

Earlier for backward classes, there was no provision for legislature reservation, nor were reservations in government in government jobs and educational seats mandated by the constitution. Thus there was no provision of reservation for the OBC's in the central government services.

As per the two above backward classes commission was established in order uplift backward classes. First backward classes commission was appointed in 1953 under the chairman of Kaka Saheb Kalelkar. The commission submitted its report in March 1955. It identified 2399 backward classes and 837 were declared or most backward.On December 20, 1978 under the chairmanship of B.P Mandal the backward classes' commission was appointed by the Janta government. It identified 3743 castes comprising 52 percent of the population of India as "Other backward classes". it submitted report in 1980.

On August 7, 1990 the Prime Minister Mr. V. P. SINGH announced the implementation of the Mandal commission recommendation. Seats should be reserved for OBC students in all scientific, technical and professional institution run by the central as well as state government as it was recommended. The quantum of reservation should be the same as in the government services (i.e.) 27 percent.

Backward class people is a collection term used by the government of India for castes which are economically and socially backward and face, or may have faced discrimination on ground of birth. Majority of them do not have any land ownership or economic independence and are dependent or forward castes for employment, mostly as farm hands or mental labor, or derive income from self-employment on caste-dependent skill assignment. They live mainly in rural India and perform hard physical labor like agriculture work. Backward castes constitute around 50 percent of the Indian population. So to uplift this half population of reservation is provided to them in educational and employment sectors.

Getting Benefit by Backward Castes or Not

Reservation policy is meant for the benefit of the depressed groups in the society. OBC's reservation meant for the provision of benefits to the backward classes in India. But, the most of them who did not know about the reservation and quota how can be they will get benefitted from it. So, it is necessary to make the people aware about the reservation for OBC's. Those who were further asked that when and how they got benefits. Here, the study shows that most of their negative response on that.

Time of Benefit and how they can get it

No doubt, there is rare now still know their reservation rights. If there is knowledge of quota seats how can they get benefit. With this there is no possibility that when they get benefit. It is not possible there to get time of benefit because members of them still are not able to get benefit. And, there is no question left that how the OBC respondent's get benefit because there are little who know about quota seats and who know quota seats are not able to get any benefit from it due to lesser chances of any support . So here is no one/single one eligible to answer this question.

Regarding Continuing Reservation

Those who frame the constitution made a reservation provision for the Scheduled Caste and Scheduled Tribes and Other Backward classes also, who are perceived by the government to be inadequately represented in the services and institution. So it was made the provision for the special class to ensure reservation. According to this majority of them should do favor in regarding these useful step but, most of them here raise voice to do not able to achieve the benefit due to non- availability of Other Backward Caste Certificate.

Table – 2

Should reservation policy continue?

S. No.	Should reservation continue (categories)	Number	Percentage
1.	Yes	46	92.00
2.	Can't say	04	08.00
	Total	**50**	**100.0**

Initially it was only for a ten year period but after every subsequent time it was extended for 60 years through constitutional amendment. The 93rd constitutional amendment brings for ensuring reservation to Other Backward Classes, Scheduled Castes and Scheduled Tribe. OBC's view about the continuation of reservation policy that nearly 92 per cent respondents favor its continuation only nearly 8 per cent which also includes those who are unaware of the reservation replied that they cannot say anything with regards to its continuation.

Issues and Problems in the Sociology of Jammu & Kashmir

Favouration of Reservation Continuation

Reservation policy is for the benefits of the deprived backward people or classes in the society. There will no one who cannot want to avail opportunities given in the reservation policy to upgrade his status in the local hierarchy.

Table-3

Reason in favor of reservation continuation

S.no.	REASONS	NUMBER	PERCENTAGE
1.	Overall beneficial to poor	20	40.00
2.	Uplift the position of poor	11	22.00
3.	For the rights of the poor	17	34.00
4.	For future benefit of the poor	06	12.00
5.	Achievement of status	05	10.00
6.	These facilities should continue	05	10.00
7.	Could not give any reason	04	08.00
8.	Better child future	03	06.00
9.	Helpful	02	04.00
10	With better and transparent implementation	02	04.00
11.	Helps in bringing equality	02	04.00
	Total	**50**	**100.0**

Everyone whosever get this opportunity of getting benefit generally tries to get it. There are reasons that why the most of them want the continuation of the reservation policy. Nearly 40 percent says that it is beneficial to poor. Those persons who say that it is to uplift the status of the poor constitute 22.00 per cent says that it is the right of the poor and 34 percent says that it is the rights of the poor. Some who said that it is for future benefit of the poor i.e. 12.00 percent. Few give importance for achievement of status and should these facilities be continuing are 10 and 10 per cent. Another some 08 per cent could not give any reason and 06 percent those who given view about the better child future was 06 per cent. At last, only 12 per cent said about the helpful, with better and transparent implementation and helps in bringing equality reasons.

Fulfillment with Reservation Policy

In the present scenario of the country there is hue and shout about the current reservation policy. There are reservation and anti-reservation opposite in the country. There are sections of people who are most mollified with the existing reservation policy and there are those who get benefit from the reservation policy.

Issues and Problems in the Sociology of Jammu & Kashmir

Table-4

Scope of satisfaction with the surviving reservation strategy

S.No.	Extent of satisfaction	Number	Percentage
1.	Satisfied	21	42.00
2.	Least satisfied	19	38.00
3.	Most satisfied	05	10.00
4.	No response	05	10.00
	Total	**50**	**100.0**

There people who are beneficial from the reservation policy are in full support its continuation. Nearly 42.00 percent of them are satisfied with reservation policy. The people who want to improve it further and least satisfied constitute 38.00 percent of the respondent. Only,10 percent did not able to give any response regarding their satisfaction with the existing reservation policy perhaps they were too suppressed to avail the benefit and those most satisfied about the existing reservation benefit was also 10 per cent.

Reasons against the reservation policy

There are some of them those who have straightly opposite view point regarding the reservation. Role of the reservation policy to be uplift the status of the poor masses but in actual sense the benefit of this policy does not grabbed by the needy ones. Moreover, this condition so worst in the state- Jammu and Kashmir. There no quota is given on the OBCs in the state as is case in other parts of the country and in J & K OBC nomenclature has been changed to OSC. Under this category 2 percent quota is given and not 27 percent as in case with other parts of country. Majority of people deprived from their right from last 22 years after the implementation of 27 percent quote for them in the state and central institutions.

References

- Ahuja, Ram, 1999, Indian Social Systems, Rawat publication Jaipur and New Delhi.
- Anand, Balwant Singh, The Sikhs and Sikhism, Sikh Gurudwara Management Committee, Delhi.
- Cohn (Eds), Structure and Change in Indian Society, Rawat Publications, Jaipur and New Delhi: 189-200.
- Dumont, Louis, 1970. Homo Hierarch us: The Caste System and its implications, Weidenfeld and Niclson, London.
- Gill Man Mohan S, perception of reservation as a mean of Social Justice, Guru Nanak Dev, Journal of Sociology 22(2), Oct 2001; p 99-111
- Ghurya, G.S., 1969 "Caste and Race in India, Bombay Popular Prakashan.
- Ibbertson, D., Punjab caste, Neeraj Publishing House, Delhi, p 237 Indian Human Development Report 1999, OUP , Delhi, 1999.
- India Development Report, Oxford University Press, Delhi, 1999-2000.
- Judge, Paramjit S. and Bal, Gurpreet. Understanding the Paradox of changes among in Punjab EPW, 43(41), 2008(11-Oct), p49-55 Mershman, Paul, 1981.Punjabi kinship and Marriage. Hindustan Publishing Corporation, Delhi.
- Kumar, Sanjay et al, 2002."Changing Pattern of Social Mobility: Some trends over time", Economic and Political Weekly, 37:40:4091-4096.
- ....2002a "Determinant of Social mobility in India", Economic and Political Weekly 37:29:2984-2987.
- Macaulife, Mac Arthur 1909, The Sikh religion Vol.1 Oxford at the Clarendon Press, London.
- Singh. K.S 1998. India's Communities Vol.6 Oxford University Press New Delhi
- Rose, H.A., 1919 "Glossary of the Tribe and caste of the Punjab and North Province", Volume II, Amar Prakashan: Delhi.
- Srinivas, M.N., 1956 "A note on Sanskritization and Westernization", For Eastern Quarterly Review, 15: 481-495.
- ....1966 "Social Change in Modern India", Allied Publishers, Bombay.
- ....1996 "Mobility in the caste system", In Milton Singer and Bernard S.

Webliography

1.   "The Tribune, Chandigarh, India - Main News". Tribuneindia.com. Retrieved 2012-09-21.
2.   Anand, Arun (24 May 2006). "What is India's population of other backward classes?". Archived from the original on 26 May 2007.
3.   "Supreme Court stays OBC quota in IITs, IIMs". *rediff.com* (Rediff.com India Limited). 29 March 2007. Retrieved 2007-04-01.
4.   "New Cutoff for OBCs". *The Telegraph*. 11 April 2008. Retrieved 2008-04-11.
5.   NCBC Central list of Other Backward Classes
6.   http://articles.timesofindia.indiatimes.com/2006-11-01/india/27792478_1_obc-count-obc-numbers-nsso
7.   "About Us - Brief History". Socialjustice.nic.in. Retrieved 2012-09-21.
8.   "Ministry of Social Welfare Resolution". *Gazette of India*. New Delhi. 10 September 1993. pp. ?–52. Retrieved 24 March 2013.
9.   Kumar, D Suresh (25 September 2010). "17 yrs after Mandal, 7% OBCs in govt jobs". *Times News Network*. Archived from the original on 27 October 2010. Retrieved 27 October 2010.
10.   "The Tribune, Chandigarh, India - Main News". Tribuneindia.com. Retrieved 2012-09-21.
11.   Anand, Arun (24 May 2006). "What is India's population of other backward classes?". Archived from the original on 26 May 2007.
12.   "Supreme Court stays OBC quota in IITs, IIMs". *rediff.com* (Rediff.com India Limited). 29 March 2007. Retrieved 2007-04-01.
13.   "New Cutoff for OBCs". *The Telegraph*. 11 April 2008. Retrieved 2008-04-11.
14.   NCBC Central list of Other Backward Classes

Other links

- *Ministry of Social Justice & Empowerment, Government of India*
- *National Commission for Backward Classes, central list by state*
- *Government Gazettes for Central Government List of OBC at SocialJustice.nic.in*
- *OBCReservation.net*
- *OBCguru.com*

CHAPTER-IV

THE MENACE OF BEGGING IN THE CITIES OF KASHMIR

A SOCIOLOGICAL ANALYSIS

SHABEER AHMAD BHAT

Introduction

Begging is an issue, which was not given much attention so far. In particular, the problem of beggary has been studied in the context of the problems and the sociology of homeless men (Anderson 1961; Hope and Young 1986). Regarding developing countries, available data on this subject reflect Indian conditions in a relatively greater extent. But, even in India there was no comprehensive study of the subject. The first available book based on Indian conditions is the book edited by Kumarappa (1945) entitled "The Beggar Problem in India". It is basically geared towards the living conditions and the causation of beggary in the city of Bombay. Similar projects were taken up and completed in Delhi and Madras. Recently, the Aligarh Muslim University conducted a survey among beggars in Kerala. The researches that have been undertaken so far are mostly in the form of local fact-finding studies like Begging the Concept, Causes, Categories and Lives of Beggars.

Begging is generally viewed as an activity emanated from poverty and destitution. It is practiced to obtain from others what one is unable to get by oneself. It is a request directed to the rest of the society to bring oneself out of misery and poverty. In this regard, MOLSA (1992:2) defined begging as a method of earning one's living from the income obtained from other sectors of society using age, health and economic conditions as a means of gaining sympathy. Begging, according to Webster's Third New International Dictionary (1976:198) is practiced especially habitually for the same reasons given by MOLSA. The encyclopedia of social work in India (1968:47) viewed beggars as mobile charity seeker people who could easily be noticed by the way they live and earn money essential for survival; and most of who are homeless and live in the open or in the impoverished huts.

The definition of a beggar as given in the European vagrancy act is quoted in Encyclopedia of Social Work in India (1968:49) and reads, "A beggar means any person of European extraction found asking for alms when he has sufficient means of subsistence or asking for alms in a threatening or insolent manner or continuing to ask for alms of any persons, after he has been required to desist." In his book entitled "the Sociology of Homeless Man" Anderson (1961) included beggars in the group of homeless migratory and casual workers. In the study which has pictured the life and the problems of the group of homeless migratory and casual workers in Chicago, Anderson (1961) divided the homeless men into five groups: (a) the seasonal laborer, (b) the migratory, casual laborer, the hobo, (c) the migratory, non-worker, the tramp, (d) the non-migratory, casual laborer, the so called "home guard," and (e) the bum. Groups b, c, d and e constitute what are known in economic writings "The Residuum of Industry". For Anderson (1961) the seasonal worker, the hobo, and the tramp are the migratory types; the home guard and the bum are relatively stationary. The home guard, like the hobo is a casual laborer, but he works, often only by the day, now at one and again at another of the multitude of unskilled jobs. The bum like the tramp is unwilling to work and lives by begging and petty theft. The bum, are men who are wholly or partially dependent and frequently diligent as well. The most hopeless and the most helpless of all the homeless men is the bum. Old, helpless, and unemployable, these are the most pitiable, the most repulsive types of the down-and - outs. In general, the tramp and the bum constitute beggars.

Nevertheless, the concept of begging can have various definitions based on the type of people engaged in the activity and the purposes of begging. Some beg as a ritual, others may have religious reasons while the majority, were drifted to the activity because of economic or social reasons (MOLSA, 1992:3). For the purpose of this study, however, the concept of begging or beggary can be conceptualized as an act of asking alms as a means of livelihood and hence is essential for survival. It is not possible to attribute begging to a single cause. According to Anderson (1961), the conditions and motives that make people homeless in general and beggar in particular may be classified into five main heads: (a) unemployment and seasonal work, (b) the misfits of industry, whether due to physical handicaps, mental deficiency, occupational diseases, or lack of vocational training (c) defects of personality as feeble mindedness, constitutional inferiority, or egocentricity which lead to the conflict of the person with constituted authority in industry, society, and government (d) crisis in the life of the person as family conflicts, misconduct and crime, which exile a man from home and community and detach him from normal social ties, (e) racial or national discrimination where race, nationality or social class of the person enters as a factor of adverse selection for employment and (f) wanderlust-the desire for new experience, excitement, and adventure, which moves the boy to 'see the world'.

According to the report of MOLSA (1992), the main reasons for the majority of beggars to depend on the practice are disability, destitution during old age, unemployment and underemployment. But a variety of other reasons which include shortage of money for transportation after a visit to relatives or after medical treatment; shortage of money for medical treatment; detention for a long time; loss of money as a result of theft or robbery are also reported by most. Moorthy (1959:48) as cited in the Encyclopedia of Social Work in India provides a more or less exhaustive list of causes to begging. The causes have been discovered in a research or survey conducted in Greater Bombay. The causes include: Overpopulation in the region with consequent pressure on land and inability of land to support the people; systems of land tenure and subdivision of holdings coupled with large families and unprofitable methods of farming; debts; famines, floods and epidemics which weaken the community or impose hardships on it; family breakdowns; emotional and economic disabilities imposed on a man or a woman after desertion; chronic and pernicious diseases; physical and mental handicaps; truancy and delinquency; inability to secure a job; unwillingness to work; religious bias and vows and binding one to the mendicant order; anti-social attitudes and child lifting's; lack of facilities for training for employment; lack of institutions providing for the welfare of the unattached, abandoned and disabled; lack of social security measures and absence of social responsibility; obvious attractions of city life, linked up with possibility of easy and ticket less railway travel, and the general outlook on age which inclines one to believe in destiny. As Moorthy (1959) argues in every aspect of begging some of these causes would be found to be operating. Besides, the problem being more urban in character has roots in the socio-economic conditions prevailing in the country and concerns itself with a large numbers of handicapped persons besides the able bodied professional beggars.

The causes for begging can only be clearly identified through research that takes into account individual cases and those who have experienced it. Official statistics and reports may not depict the magnitude and underlying causes for begging. It is therefore important to utilize individual case studies to depict the underlying causes and the different factors associated with begging in its local and national contexts. Besides, the causes of begging can be given different interpretations and justifications from the viewpoint of different people and interest groups. Thus, the thesis attempted to show that if sufficient individual cases are examined, and if the situation is framed in the larger historical and socio economic context, the circumstances of the beggars can proved to be more problematic than has been assumed heretofore. The actor's point of view was considered to be crucial in order to avoid stereotypes and hasty generalizations. In an aim to give some clue

to the measures required to control the problem, Encyclopedia of Social Work in India (1968:46-47) classified beggars into the following categories:
1) Those who beg because they can not work on account of old age,
2) Those who beg because they are permanently disabled or infirm or chronically ill or otherwise handicapped (including children who beg because they are physically or mentally handicapped or are destitute or are without proper guardianship), and 3) Those who though able bodied, beg because of unemployment or underemployment or to earn livelihood by easy means. In a similar way, Anderson (1961:102) divided beggar types into the able-bodied and the nonable- bodied. The non-able bodied beggars are more numerous in the cities. They are forced because of their handicaps, to remain where the greater numbers of people are. Some handicapped beggars, however, are able to travel with marvelous speed over the country. These non-able-bodied types as Anderson (1961:102) go by different names according to their afflictions. Peggy is a one-legged man. Stumpy is a legless man. Swingy is a man with one or both arms off. Blink is a man with one or both eyes defected. A dummy is a man who is dumb or a deaf and dumb. Some of these types do not beg. They make a livelihood by peddling or working at odd jobs. A nut is a man who is apparently mentally deranged.

According to a report made by MOLSA (1992:6-9) three different types of beggars are believed to have existed and still continue to exist in Ethiopia. The first category of beggars includes the disabled, the aged and other destitute, who ask for alms around churches, mosques, public places and rural villages. The second category includes the Orthodox religious students and professional beggars known as H*minas* or *Lalibelas*. The third category includes holly beggars of various sorts including priests who carry sacred pictures and ask for charity for different reasons. The major concern of this research paper is to through light on some practical aspects of begging in general and begging in the valley of Kashmir in particular. One gets some glimpses of the way beggars live, earn and spend money from research reports and some of the limited books. According to Encyclopedia of Social Work in India (1968:47), the surveys in India reveal the following conditions with respect to the lives of the beggars. The income of a beggar in different parts of the country varies Most of the beggars are homeless and live in the open or in the impoverished huts. Some of them are married. Quite a percentage of the male and female beggars live as married without formal solemnization of marriage. In the rank of beggars, there are the aged, the infirm, the chronically ill, mentally ill, vagrants, patients of leprosy, patients of T.B, Juveniles, etc. The methods they employ while begging are plain appeal, singing and dancing, exposing sores, etc. Most of the expenditure they incur is on food, smoking and entertainment. Intoxicating drugs account for the remaining expenditure. Some, who do not earn much, live on collected waste food. A large number of beggars are illiterate but there are some who have received primary and even secondary education. The large number of beggars lives on the charity of citizens. Some of the beggars or indigent persons are taken care of in institutions, but this number is negligible as would appear from the review of homes and services established to help the beggars. The traditional way of giving charity has as a matter of fact encouraged the able-bodied beggars to take advantage of it with the genuinely needy. Religion has also, to some extent, given sanction to the profession of begging. According to the same report, those who have become beggars out of misfortune, disease or handicaps, are often treated as social outcasts. They are often the victims of social stigmatization. Professional beggars are probably the creation of indiscriminate charity.

The survey results conducted by MOLSA in 1992 have also shown a more or less similar conditions pertaining to the lives of beggars. Accordingly, the following conclusions were reached, which explain some local facts regarding the beggar problem and lives of beggars: (1) a large number of beggars are migrants And the majority have very low educational and employment status, (2) most of the migrant beggars came from the northern regions which are affected by natural and man made disasters, (3) high proportion of beggars resort to begging within the years 1990 and 1991 owing to economic and socio-political situations which include escalating cost of living and displacement, (4) beggars who are engaged in activities other than begging in order to supplement their income are engaged in marginalized jobs, (5) beggars earn better income than other urban poor or minimum large earners in the country, (6) family disruption through death, divorce or unknown reasons contribute to child begging.

Begging in the valley of Kashmir

Dispelled from the normal social and family life, they are made to engage their life in others mercy. Beggary, once regarded as a huge social problem in Kashmir, become all the more baffling with the numbers diminishing. There was a time when we could see them everywhere from the market place to roads to temples but with the socio-economic development they've become a rare commodity. From a community which created nuisance to the public have increasingly become rare and if they are traceable they are in better pastures with a paradigm shift in their dress, behaviour and modus operandi of begging. Effective anti beggary laws, frequent raids by the Corporation authorities and positive approach taken by the "Child Line" have reduced their numbers. The remaining few no longer do begging near road side pavements, traffic lights and under flyovers. This gave way to better and neat environment. The thin line that differentiates beggars from the lower middle class is getting slimmer as they too lead an almost normal family life. The study found inadequate social security measures as the major reason for contemporary begging. If we are able to adopt and implement social insurance and old age pension schemes at grass root level we would be able to abolish this menace from the society to a large extent. It is interesting to note the drastic changes seen over the last 3-4 years with regard to their appearance, life style, places of beggary and even the reason for begging.

b) Places where they were found in the cities

Places	Percentage
Bus stands/Railway Stations	17 %
Market Places	6 %
Tourist spots	10 %
Religious Places	67 %
Total	100%

c) The reasons for the beggary

Causes	Percentage
Old age	15%
Chronic diseases	6%
Poverty	15%
Under the shade of religion	42%
Profession	5%
Total 100	100%

Issues and Problems in the Sociology of Jammu & Kashmir

d) Nativity of the beggars

No. States	Number Percentage
Kashmiries	62%
Non Kashmiries	38%
Total 100	100%

Major findings of the study

1. A major finding of the study is their dwindling numbers.
2. Forced beggary has almost reduced.
3. Push factors like old age, disability, chronic illness are the major reasons.
4. Beggars in Pilgrim places operate in two schedules. From morning to afternoon they sit in front of the temples/ churches/ mosques and after taking the free meal (annadaanam) they generally go for home / shop begging. This pattern is generally seen among non Kashmiri beggars.
5. Numbers of beggars from other states have increased significantly in numbers due to light vigilance by the authorities of the state.
6. Concentration areas have been limited to religious places.
7. Many of them are chronically ill and carriers of many diseases.
8. Use of drugs is also visible and sometimes they work as agents for drug trafficking.
9. Women beggars are comparatively higher in number.
10. There is no regional difference between three cities (Srinagar, Anantnag and Kulgam in life styles and begging pattern.
11. Many outside Kashmiries have left the state as they were caught by the Jammu and Kashmir Police in many anti social activities like alcohol sellers etc.
12. Number of individual child beggars has also significantly increased.
13. Mother/Father beggar with child has also decreased.
14. Because of the hospitable and religious nature of kashmiries most of the beggars find this valley a shield against their homelessness and this social problem is increasing day by day.
15. With in the month of Ramadan the valley of Kashmir turned into the house of beggars and almost every religious place be it mosque ot any other religious shrine all places are found to be covered by beggars at large throughout the month.

Major changes taken place over the last Five years

1) Changes in their appearance

Issues and Problems in the Sociology of Jammu & Kashmir

Majority of the beggars are having normal dress code, which is similar to persons belonging to lower middle class life. Shabby and torn clothes gave way to normal dress. We can recognize them only if they are engaged in begging.

2) Significant increase in their numbers

The reasons behind increasing number of beggars may be,

a) Ineffective implementation of anti beggary law.

b) Frequent raid by the corporation.

c) Fear of the Police.

d) Positive approach taken by the "Child Line" to rehabilitate children.

e) Anti social activities and related imprisonment.

3) Majority of them are aged, disabled and having chronically ill.

4) Numbers of professional beggars have reduced drastically.

5) Majority of them have been moved from road sides, railway stations, bus stands to religious places.

6) Child beggars seen mainly in the railway station premises and mostly they are non Kashmiries.

7) "Mother & Child" beggars have almost vanished.

8) Beggars are hardly traceable in the tourist spots.

9) Generally people donate denomination of money between 2 to 10 rupees; interestingly the paisa coins lost its charm and relevance.

Religious Centers and the Beggary

Nowadays religious centers have turned to be a safe haven for the beggars. This is the place where they get money, food and also safe shelter. Nobody questions them or do not disturb them from begging. One cannot demarcate between a beggar and a religious devotee. Being a religious place they are safe and they use this place as shield to their activities. The strong protection of religion may invite more beggars to religious spots in future. The law enforcing authority can't question them and having the protection of religion more beggars may come to these places in huge numbers in future. In religious places giving and taking alms are without considering the physical ailment. There is no room for sympathetic drive because disability assessment is hardly done in these places. People give alms as a part of religious ceremony. As they give alms as a part of their religious ceremony and they do give alms to satisfy their devotional drive, able bodied beggars can also earn. Begging around the religious places is more profitable because they need to spend only a little time in front of the temple i.e morning 8.00 am to 11.00 am (3 hours) during which visitors come to visit the temples. They earn alms between Rs. 200-500 at an average per day, (the range is determined by the class of the religious place).

The range goes very high, though rarely during seasons of festivals / pilgrimage.

This revenue is a steady income and even much more than the welfare pension given by the state government. Free meals provided by the temples (annadaanam) have encouraged them to stick on to these places normally. The number of beggar increase during festival season or special ceremony days of the shrines take place. We were able to see around 45 beggars around the 'Hazratbal shrine on the days of religious festivals which are Islamic in nature. It is difficult to differentiate these people from the normal devotee as these beggars gel with other thoroughly. Their physical manners and appearance do not match as that of ordinary beggars. Such beggars generally return to their original places as soon as the festival is over.

Rehabilitation

All the more important is the need for a constant watch by the police and worship place authorities on the increasing inflow of beggars, particularly during festival seasons and other auspicious days and occasions. A separate vigilance squad may be able to face the untoward action that is likely to happen behind begging.

Proper, systematic and scientific rehabilitation is the only solution by which they could be taken back to the society. A government agency alone cannot make it a success without proper involvement of NGOs and the public. The government should come out with rehabilitation schemes for the beggars with participation of the public (as donation). Able bodied men and women should be encouraged to work. More contribution should come in this direction to have a proper rehabilitation programme.

The old and the infirm should be provided with shelter and special care with proper medical facility in rehabilitation homes if possible. Religious institutions and charitable societies should be delegated to rehabilitate them.

A practical income generating programme should be made effective in the home to make them self sufficient and engage them in some physical work. Programmes like, rabbit farming, poultry farming, fish farms are feasible depending upon the market conditions. Concerned corporations and the LSGD's should design a comprehensive plan for a suitable place, a proper marketing strategy and mustering of funds for this purpose. Sponsorships are very uncommon in the rehabilitation centers of beggars when compared to other orphanages in around the cities where we focused our study. It is quite unfortunate.

Suggestions

1. The anti beggary laws should be made and implemented effectively throughout the valley.
2. Instead of starting campaigns against beggary awareness camps should be organized by both govt. and non govt. organizations periodically.
3. Proper use of Radio, TV, and other means of communication should be used to make people a wear on daily basis.
4. Jammu and Kashmir police should be empowered to take action beggars throughout the state.
5. Lost but not the least the authorities should come forward and should know the main cause of begging and accordingly should provide socio, and economic support to beggars in order to remove this social evil.
6. Govt. should make a package for the local beggars under which a Rupees of 1500-2000 should be given to those who are in need of it and an anti begging movement should be stared for those who are outside beggars.

Refrences

1. Adedibu AA (1989). "Begging and Poverty In Third World Cities: A case study of Ilorin, Nigeria" Ilorin J. Bus. Soc. Sci. (IJBSS), 1: 25 – 40.
2. Akinbola GE (2002). "Poverty Reduction through the Crop Sub-sector in Nigeria: A Regional Perspective" in Okunmadewa, F.Y.(ed), Poverty Reduction and the Nigeria
3. Becker H (1963). "Outsiders". New York: Free Press
4. Burgess E (1925). "The Growth of the City" in Robert E. Park, Ernest W.
5. Burgess and Roderick D. Mckerzie (eds) The City. Chicago University of Chicago Press
6. Cuff EC, Sharrock WW, Francis DW (1990). "Perspectives in Sociology" 3rd edition. Boston: Unwin Hyman
7. Dahrendorf R (1959). "Towards a Theory of Social Conflict" J. Conflict Resolut. 2 (june), pp. 170 – 183
8. Egeonu D (1988). "Sick Beggars Pose Health Hazard" Sunday Times, April 17, pp. 8-9.
9. Esan OI (2009). "Panhandlers as Rhetors: Discourse Practices of
10. Peripatetic Beggars in Southwestern Nigeria"

CHAPTER-V

ASPIRATIONS OF EDUCATED GIRLS IN RURAL INDIA

THE CASE OF JAMMU AND KASHMIR

GOWHER AHMAD SHALLA

INTRODUCTION

Ultimately she is taught to sacrifice her self either as a mother or a wife. She is treated as an inferior human being. She has to be governed by social norms prescribed by the male dominated society to be treated as a burden on parents and deprived of opportunities in life. She faces oppressions and suppressions (Kulshreshtha, 1991). As stated by Simone de Behaviour (cited from Tandon, 2008) in her book "second sex" "one is not born but rather becomes a woman. No biological, psychological or economic fate determines the figure that human female presents in society, it is civilization as a whole that produces this create intermediate between male and eunuch, which is described as feminine."

Education makes the women and girls aware about their rights and they have the desire of success in the traditionally male dominated field. Education is a human right and it is only through education that the goals of equality, development and peace can be achieved in the society. Education is a major instrument of social change which is necessary for development and nation building. Education without discrimination benefits both boys and girls and thus contributes towards the equal relationship between men and women. Education of women is important as it improves the health, nutrition and education of family besides ensuring women's participation in the decision making process of the family and society at large (Mohit, 2005). The equality among human and across the societies can be achieved only by providing sufficient and equal opportunities for better health and education to the girls and women. It is through primary education that women are able to overcome the social and traditional barriers and promote social development, while by achieving higher education, promotion of social and occupational mobility, personality development and intellectual development is possible among Women folk (Rameshwari and Varsha, 2007).

It is only through education that the gateways of peace, progress and development for people especially women whether living in rural or urban areas can be achieved. Education makes the women aware about the discrimination, injustice, ill-treatment which they are facing over decades. Education create the desire among the girls to participate in the welfare policies and programmes which improve the living standard of people especially women living in rural areas and remove the backwardness which women are facing from the very beginning. Educated girls wish to flourish themselves in every field of society same as that of men and overcome the norms, rules and regulations set up for them by men folk in the society. They tend to raise their status in the society by having access to resources especially in the field of education, health, media, employment, marketing, administration and other opportunities. They also have the desire to use their skills and creative energy in the development process and create social and political identity same as that of men. Education fills them with the aspirations to liberate themselves from the bondage of slavery in the society and aware the people about the contribution which they are making for the society. Not only men but women also have the right of financial autonomy, freedom of movement, participation in the household decisions etc. Education enables them to throw away the un-equal, inferior and weak status bestowed upon them by the society. Educated women have better job prospects and thus have a greater value outside the home. They marry later, have fewer children and are better able to influence family decisions and overcome the silence which they bear over decades.

In this chapter the aspirations of educated girls has been described by certain parameters like age of marriage, equal inheritance rights, participation in decision making process, job preference mate selection, and so on.

Age at Marriage

The Hindu Marriage Act 1955 has brought revolution in the institution of marriage. The minimum age of the boy and the girl is fixed i.e. 18 years for girl and 21 years for boy (Chandrakala, 1969). Also the child marriage Restraint Act 1929 was amended by presenting the bill of the prohibition of child marriage Act 2006. The act was amended to make the act more effective and the punishment stricter so as to eradicate or prevent the evil practice of child marriage in the country. This will enhance the health of children and the status of women (Arora, 2008). Marriage is an important decision of life but in India the domain of marriage is decided by the parents or elderly kinsmen. In spite of strict laws against child marriage parents tend to marry off their daughters as early as possible. As stated by Ritu, Thind and Seema (2007) parents who fail to arrange the marriage of their daughters at an appropriate age are looked down upon in the society such negative sanctions have made marriage universal in India. In contrast, the society adopts a totally different attitude in case of men, e.g. they have all the liberties in mate selection and marital adjustments.

The data highlights that majority of the respondents (74.52 per cent) has reported that age of marriage should be 23 to 27 years which is followed by 22.64 per cent of the respondents who report that girls should be married off during 18 to 22 years of age (Table 5.1). Nearly 3 per cent of the respondents has reported that age of marriage should be 28 years and above.

Table 5.1: Distribution of respondents on the basis of their preference of age at marriage

Age of Marriage	No. of Respondents
18-22 years	24 (22.64)
23-27 years	79 (74.52)
28 years and above	03 (2.84)
Total	106 (100.00)

* Figures in parenthesis denote percentage

The data clearly indicates that 3/4th of the girls have the desire to marry after attaining age of 23 to 27 years, so that they will not face any problem in the completion of their studies. It may be also concluded that education makes girls conscious of their carrier which in turn ensures their successful and happy married life.

Equal Inheritance Rights

The Indian society is a traditional society and people of India have firm faith in the laws of its Shastras. The position of women which was assigned by Narada, Vashistha and Manu etc is prevailing even today. The great sages, in their text, presented women as a dependent entity, without having any independent rights of their own. The father protects a woman in her childhood, the husband during her youth and the son in the old age. These women have no rights of independence. According to Sarvadhikari (cited from Raka, 1999), the principles of Hindu traditional law (1880) pointed out the reason for women's exclusion from inheritance. He has reported that according to these sages women are unfit to acquire property as they are prone to affection, kindness and many types of soft sentiments. Thus women will never be able to manage the property.

Although constitutions of India has provided fundamental rights to everybody irrespective of caste, creed, sex, colour but the women are denied from the fundamental right of acquisition of property. Indian parliament made several bills/acts in the last four decades to bless the women with more power and authority and bestow her benefits, and those acts are Hindu Succession Act (1956), Hindu Minority and Guardianship Act (1956), Hindu Adoption and Maintenance Act (1956). The main target of these acts has been to create greater equality among both sexes. But unfortunately, these acts and provisions are present in theory not into practice. Consequently, even today the Indian women's rights are governed by traditional norms which treat them unequally. Muslims are not away from it, though it is mentioned in the Holy Quran to give equal inheritance to women also, but Muslim women are denied such rights. They have the desire to own property but all their desires and aspiration remains as a dream which never full-fill and in this way they are denied from their basic right and all the property is provided to sons only.

Data highlights that almost 85 per cent of the respondents has reported that they have the desire to get equal share of parental property; same as that of the male members of the family (Table 5.2). Only a small proportion of the respondents (15.09 per cent) have reported that they do not wish to get any share in the parental property.

Table 5.2: Desire to provide equal inheritance

Equal inheritance	No. of respondents
Yes	90 (84.91)
No	16 (15.09)
Total	106 (100.00)

Except the few, girls mostly have the desire to get a share of parental property. They hold that such property right may help them to be self-sufficient and tackle the problems which they are facing in the society.

Reasons for Equal Inheritance

The data with regard to the reasons given by respondents reveals that majority of the respondents (60 per cent) has stated that it is their fundamental right to get an equal share in the property of their parents; therefore they should not be denied this right of property by the parents or other family members (Table 5.3). In the view of 24.45 per cent of the respondents, getting share in the property of parents make the girls self sufficient and independent. In addition, such right in the property can help them to face the hardships of life easily and ensure their good life. Besides this, 15.55 per cent of the respondents have reported that Islam has given equal rights to both boys and girls; therefore, it becomes compulsory for the parents to treat equally girls as well as boys and provide their daughters with equal share in the property.

Table 5.3: Reasons for equal inheritance

Reasons for equal Inheritance	No. of Respondents
Islam allows	14 (15.55)
To make girls self-sufficient	22 (24.45)
Fundamental right	54 (60)
Total	90 (100.00)

* Figures in parenthesis show percentage

From the above, it may be made out that education arouse the girls awareness about the right which are bestowed upon them by the religion and the Constitution. They have the desire that their rights should be recognized and fulfilled by the parents and the society at large. Education may have attributed to their realization of the inequality that they are facing not only outside the family but also within the family.

Reasons for not giving Equal Inheritance

There are many reasons which ensure the girls un-acceptance of parental property like fear of gossiping by the people about the girls who are getting share in parental property and in this way they try to avoid the circumstances which make them talk of the village. Many girls have threat that demanding share of property becomes the cause of their disrespect in the family because they think girls do not have any right to own the property.

The data in this regard shows that 43.75 per cent respondents has reported that getting share in the property becomes the cause of disrespect in the parental family and after marriage they will not get warm welcome by the parents as well as by brothers and even parents and brothers will not allow them to visit their house (Table 5.4). This threat among girls ensures the denial of claiming their share in parental property and they do not even dare to think about it. According to 31.25 per cent of the respondents, it is the right of brothers to have/own the property of parents and girls have nothing to do with it. They further expressed that their parents are providing them shelter, provide all possible facilities and also make arrangements for their marriage besides dowry so parents should not be compelled for share in property. According to them, it is a sin to claim share in property. Further, 25 per cent of the respondents have reported that if they demand their right to property they are looked down and stigmatized/labeled as immoral in the society, so they refrain from such activities which raise fingers against them in the society.

Table 5.4: Reasons for not giving equal inheritance

Reasons	No. of Respondents
Disrespect in family	7 (43.75)
Brothers right	5 (31.25)
Lose status in society	4 (25.00)
Total	16 (100.00)

* Figures in Parenthesis denote percentage

The above data clearly depicts that girls who do not want a share in parental property feel a threat of loss of status in the family as well as in the biradari and society. Moreover, despite their willingness, they refrain to ask for their rights due to the environment in which they live and are socialized. In this way, they are denied the property right which is bestowed upon them not only by the Constitution but also by the religion.

Job preference of Educated Rural Girls

Employment of women paves their way for integration in the process of national development. Employments make the women self-sufficient and raise their status in the society. Teaching profession is the most preferred job as per the opinion of 59.43 per cent of the respondents (Table 5.10).The educated girls like teaching profession because their parents and other family members have similar liking for this profession. They also expressed that only teaching profession is good for women because in this profession they have not to spend the nights outside and also get the chance to serve the family members well. Almost 17 per cent of the respondents have reported that they like the medical profession and wish to flourish themselves in the field of medicine. Moreover, 12.26 per cent of the respondents have stated that they like to take up the administration jobs such as IAS (Indian Administrative Service), IFS (Indian Forestry Service) KAS (Kashmir administrative Service). Only 11.32 per cent of the respondents have expressed their preference for law profession largely in the area of judiciary rather than practice.

Table 5.10: Job preference of respondents

Job Preference	No. of Respondents
Teaching	63 (59.43)
Doctor/Medicine	18 (16.99)
Administrative services	13 (12.26)
Lawyer (judiciary)	12 (11.32)
Total	106 (100.00)

*Figures in parenthesis denote percentage

From the above it may be concluded that the main preference for Job is teaching as in this profession there is no need to spend the nights away from the family. Other jobs preferred by the educating girls include medicine, administration and law, though their proportion is less than those who preferred to be in the teaching line.

Marriage Preference/Choice

The data with regard to the marriage preference of the respondents is concerned a large proportion of the respondents (63.20 per cent) want to marry the spouse of their choice and not according to the parents and other family members as well by kinsmen (Table 5.11). Those who want to marry according to the choice of parents not their own constitute 36.80 per cent of the total respondents. In their opinion, parents are the best judge to select the mate.

Table 5.11: Marriage Choice of Respondents

Marriage Preference	No. of respondents
Girls choice	67 (63.20)
Parents choice	39 (36.80)
Total	106 (100.00)

* Figures in parenthesis denote percentage

From the above it may be concluded that girls want to throw away the age old tradition of selection of spouse by parents and not taking girls interest into consideration. They wish their spouse should be according to their choice.

REFERENCES

Ariya, A. (2002). *Indian Women*, Vol. 2, New Delhi, Gyan Publishing House.

Arora, K. (2006). *Marriage and Divorce Laws* (ed.), New Delhi, Professional Publishers.

Bakshi, L.G. (1970). *Towards Better Education*, New Delhi, S. Chand and Company Ltd.

Bakshi, S.R. (2001). *Empowerment of Women and Policies of Reservation*, Jaipur, Book Enclave.

Balachandirana. G. (2007). *Women's Education and Development: East Asian Lesson for South Asia*, New Delhi, Gyan Publishing House.

Bhushan, A. (1995). "Mahila Samriddhi Yojna", *Yojna*, Vol. 39, No. 9, July.

Billington, M.F. (1973). *Women in India*, New Delhi, Amarko Book Agency.

Borain, M.P. (2000). *Empowerment of Rural Women: The Deterrents and Determinants*, New Delhi, Concept Publishing Company.

Chopra, R. and Ghosh, D. (2001). "Work Patterns of Rural Women in Central Himalays," *Economic and Political Weekly*, Vol. XXXV, No.52, Dec, 30.

Dabala B., Nayak, S. and Islam, K. (2000). *Gender Discrimination in the Kashmir Valley: A Survey of Budgam and Baramulla Districts*, New Delhi, Gyan Publishing House.

Dabala, B.A. (2007). *Multi-Dimensional Problems of Women in Kashmir*, New Delhi, Gyan Publishing House.

Das, B.K. (1991). "Women in Rural Development: The Indian Experience in Women and Development" in Kalabagh, C. (ed.), *Women and Development*, New Delhi, Discovery Publishing House.

Engineer, A.A. (1995). *Problems of Muslim Women in India*, Bombay, Orient Longman Publication.

Gandhi, M.K. (1942). *Women and Social Justice*, Ahmadabad, Navajivan Publishing House.

Gender and Education for All. (2003). *United Nations Educational Scientific and Cultural Organization (UNESCO)*, Paris.

Gill, M.S. (1994). "Women and Equality: A Case Study", *Guru Nanak Journal of Sociology*, Vol.15, No. 2.

Gill, M.S. (2003). "Women and Society: Empowering through Work" (ed.), *Punjab Society: Perspectives and Challenges*, New Delhi, Concept Publishing Company.

Hasnain, N. (2005). "Muslim in India: Caste Affinity and Social Boundaries of Backwardness" in Verma, H.S. (ed.), *The OBCs and the Ruling Classes in India*, Jaipur, Rawat Publications.

Hate, A. and Chandrakala. (1969). *The Changing Status of Women in Post Independence India*, Bangalore, Allied Publishers.

Jahan and Rownok et al. (2004). "Redefining Women's Samman: Microcrdit and Gender Relations in Rural Bangladesh," *Economic and Political Weekly*, Vol. xxxix, No.32, Aug 7-13.

Jain, A. and Tripathi, S.K. (2002). "Tribal Women Yesterday, Today and Tomorrow" in Chaube, R. and Saini, K. (ed.), *Status of Women in Rural Societies*, Madhya Pradesh, Aditya Publications.

Kumar, G.D. (2007). "Women Representation in West Bengal Panchayats" in Pandya, R. (ed.), *Women in India: Issues Perspectives and Solutions*. New Delhi, New Century Publications.

Kumar, S. et al. (2003). "Primary Education in Rural Areas", *Economic Political Weekly*, Vol. xxxviii, No. 34, Aug 23-29.

McDougall, L. (2000). "Gender Gap in Literacy in Uttar Pradesh: Question for Decentralized Educational Planning," *Economic and Political Weekly*, Vol. xxxv, No. 9, May 6-12.

Mishra, S. (1993). *Status of Women in Changing Urban Hindu Family*, New Delhi, Radha Publications.

Mohanty, R.P. Biswal, D.N. (2007). *Culture, Gender and Gender Discrimination*, New Delhi, Mittal Publishers.

Mukherjee, D. (2007). "Women's Education" in Tilak, B.G. (ed.), *Education and Development*, New Delhi, A.P.H Publishing Corporation.

CHAPTER-VI
A HISTORICAL STUDY OF CHINAR TREE IN KASHMIR (INDIA)

THE TREE OF HERITAGE

MUSHTAQ AHMAD DAR

INTRODUCTION

The home of *Bune* [Kashmiri Chinar]is Greece and North Asia. It is a favorite shade tree for the people of Greece and Romans. In early historical period the trees of Bune were found in Greenland and indigenous of eastern and northern hemisphere of Mediterranean region, north east America and Mexico. From its original habitat with the passage of time it has travelled (naturally or otherwise) to Asian sub-continent including Iran, Afghanistan, Pakistan and Western Himalayan regions of India from 6000-meter elevation above MSL to 2400 meter. And in the state of Jammu and Kashmir its optimum growth range is between 1500 to 2000 meters. In its homeland, i.e Greece it regenerates naturally along the torrents in mountainous districts[1].It can be grown fairly well in Punjab plains, if supplied with a fair amount of moisture. Trails made to cultivate it in sub-tropical zone of Jammu region have been found to be partially successful as there are some of the trees of Bune struggling sluggishly to survive in Ramban, Tilo-Talab and along the Jammu airport road and Punch and Rajouri districts. The crowns of these trees are elongated and elliptical resembling a populous tree rather than the well-formed strong spreading crown of Bune.

Issues and Problems in the Sociology of Jammu & Kashmir

The Bune is an exotic tree to the state of J&K. As exotic as defined by Oxford dictionary means plants, words, and fashions or so introduced from abroad. Abroad in respect of plant communities means such plant that has been introduced into a habitant which is not within the range of its natural distribution. This range of natural distribution may be restricted to a small zone of a particular locality or may cover a vast geographical area, passing over a number of countries with in definite elevation zone.[2]

Chinars in Kashmir.

Chinar is called Bune by us and the word is Bhawini in Sanskrit which has become sorrupt and is Bune that is a blessing Mata (Mother). Bune (Chinar) is a blessing mother considered by the inhabitants of Kashmir. Its shadow keeps us cool during summer months and its sight is pleasing to the eyes. It protects us during torrential rains. Its Botanical term is *"Platanus Orientals* (plain). Its leaves and branches shine during summer months.

The Chinar is classed number one tree and is a royal tree. Its felling is strictly prohibited by the state government. It grows at a height of 4000 to 6000 feet above from sea level. It requires cool and warm climate and soil alluvial. When winter starts in, its dried leaves are turned into charcoal and used in Kangris (Fire-Pots) which keeps us warm and for us is a defence against winter. Its account is given in Rajtharangi, "as old trees in whose hollow is fire"- I believe it, this allusion to Chinar because Chinar, when it is old gets hollow and ignites spontaneously. A thorough research is required in this connection.

Laleshwari or *Lal-Ded*, a poetess saint of Kashmir during early 14th century A.D. has mentioned of Chinar:

"Kainchan Raen Chai Shehej Booni neerew Naibur Shul Karew
Kainchan Raen Chai Bara Pathe Honee Neerew Naibat to Zang Khaiyew."

Sir Jamshid Ji, poet laurate, has given the origin of chinar and says that chinar is Iranian tree which has been imported by various countries of the world. He has mentioned in his account ZinaAvista- Herodotus, father of history tells us that chinar was sacred to Sassamian Emperors of Iran because Iranians call it 'Fazal tree' biggest tree. Rulers of Damoas Island in Meditarian decorated the grave yard of their ancestors around by these chinar trees. Later on it was planted in Sicily recovered revenue from the owners on account of it. The inhabitants would enjoy its shade to the full during picnics. It was planned in Iberian Peninsula, Spain and Portugal. These were the days according to Pliny, Greek historian; French armies were invading the Roman cities and were turning into ashes in the first century of Christian era. It was sacred in Spain and France that the growers watered it by liquor at the roots. During 6th century AD it was planted in large number in various Balkan states and north Europe. It is quite evident that the chinar was in existence and planted during the reign of Lalitaditya Muktapida (AD 707-760) in Kashmir. Some opine that Islamic propagations imported this plant in Kashmir. Emperor Jahangir gives a brief account of it in his memories, he says that it is one of the oldest trees in Kashmir and exists since ancient times. When I reached near Srinagar at Rawalpur village, it started raining torrentially. I along with other fine horse riders took shelter in one of cave holes of a chinar. My father jalal-ud-Din Abar, emperor had also taken shelter here with thirty- four persons in its hollow according to Akbar nama. I can very much infer that the chinar tree is the oldest tree in the valley of Kashmir.[3]

INTRODUCTION OF BUNE IN THE KASHMIR VALLEY:-

The common saying goes that the Bune was introduced by Mughals in the valley when Akbar annexed the valley within his domain in 1586 AD. It is a historical fact that Akbar planted about 1200 plants of Bune near the sacred shrine of Hazratbal and engaged sufficient watch and ward personal to protect the plants and would provide milk to irrigate the plants instead of water. This grove of plants later on was responsible to moderate the local season by providing a pleasant breeze on hot summer days. Observing this phenomenon Jahangir named this site as Baghi Naseem. The Mughals were in deep love with this tree because of their great aesthetic sense and planted the tree on all important routes, gardens and parks and government lands. They extended royal protection to the tree and declared it as a royal tree-which could not be cut down even if found to be growing in private lands. In the year 1619 A.D Mughal emperor Jahangir and his Queen Noor Jahan ordered planting of Bune in Shalimar garden and watched their progress of growth with interest.[4]

Mrs. Stuart Villers in her book 'Gardens Of Mughal Empire' says that emperor Jahangir important chinar trees from Iran so that his beloved queen's desire is fulfilled but this argument cannot be relied upon. He himself mentions its existence in his memories. He further says that I have brought about 800 plants fromIran and planted them at Shalimar, Mansabal, Achabal, Verinag, Kokernag (Bondu Zalgam) Shadipur and Ganderbal. In AD 1635 Emperor Shahjhan planted about 1200 chinar plants at Naseem Bagh.[5] During the reign of Aurangzeb-Alamgir, Islam Khan (Zia-ud-din Badakshi) planted chinar trees in his town, which he founded after his name Islamabad (Anantnag)which can even now be seen at Sher-Bagh and in the temples nearby. Mughal Governors held darbars under the chinar trees on a raised platform. They discussed day-to-day problems of the state under the shadow of chinars and music, dance and drama was also held. During the night chinar trees were illuminated which added the magnificence of the Darbar.[6]

Some historians have stated that it was Jahangir who named the Bune as "Chinar" when he saw a grove of Bune trees from a long distance during autumn season and was puzzled to find out if the trees were set ablaze mysteriously. Actually the phenomenon was due to scarlet (deep red) color of the leaves, which was responsible for turning the surround as if it were set on fire. Seeing this phenomenon the Mughal Emperor cried in ecstasy "chinar" (Persian word meaning 'what a fire) several times and his associates followed the suit. Thereafter the Bune was named as 'chinar' by the higher echelons of Kashmiri society, as the history of Kashmir has proved that such a people to be the great servants of their great masters, even if they may be to change their culture, their language and, even the fundamental principles of their religion. Basically the change of color of the leaves of Bune is a natural phenomenon, which occurs in autumn season on Bune tree and other trees as well (such as maples). The name 'chinar' hasn't however been accepted by masses. Some other historians negate the above story as a myth. They are of the opinion that Jahangir, seeing color of the Bune during autumn seasons uttered the Persian name of the tree-'chinar'- this name thereafter because the official name of the tree and spoken by loyalists of Kashmir as Persian was the official language of the valley at that time. It was Jahangir who put forth the concept of Char chinari, i,e planting of Bune on all four sides of park in such that a man sitting in the park will not be bothered by the hot perching rays of sun even if the sun moves from one position to other.[7]

In 1398 AD, when construction work of Jamia Masjid of Srinagar was taken in hand Sultan Zain-ul-Abdin a few years later planted a few chinar trees in its compound and around it in order to give it an aesthetic view. In A.D 1674, the mosque was destroyed on account of a big conflagration. When Aurangzeb heard of it, his first enquiry was whether the chinars were safe."Prince Dara Shukoh built a big garden of chinars at Vijbror (Bijbehara) in AD 1646-AH 1066. The chinars are still visible and extant. One of the chinar trees at Vijbror (Bijbehara) is above three hundred years old. Chinar leaves have played an important role in arts and crafts. In Papermachie and walnut works the painting of chinars are beautifully decorated. Its wood is used for making of motors, furniture and oil presses. In Kashmir our shrines, temples and tirthas and churches are decorated by planting these trees in their vacant lands nearby. It is a sacred act[8].

Issues and Problems in the Sociology of Jammu & Kashmir

At present the number of chinar trees in the valley is approximately 50000. Padshahi bagh at Bijbehara was decorated by prince Dara shukoh with chinar trees under the superintendence of Daroga Mohd.Zahid-Abdul Hassan Samarqandi. This site lies on the right and left banks of river Jhelum near the present bridge which connects Dacchin pur illaqa with that of Nandi illaqa and is now converted into a park. Near Bachhpur colony, there was an old chinar garden called Baghi-Illahi which was planted by Emperor Jahangir in 1050 AH (1640 AF-Nuri-Jehan).Planting of chinar trees was encouraged by the Mughal emperors. Nasim Bagh is entirely a chinar grove. It makes delightful camping grounds where they afford a cool and very welcome shade in the hottest part of the day. It has a place of honour among the trees of chinar has a beautiful glamour , when autumn lights up, big chinar plane trees burn red against the dark blue rock background. There are few more brilliant breathlessly interesting sights. Chinar bagh('Bohemia of Srinagar') an Isunti Khul canal is cool and shady encampment in Srinagar owes its name to its magnificent chinars. Achabal, verinag and Kokernag and Ganderbal will lose its charm if the chinars had not been planted there. Mughal Emperors extended its cultivation Jehangir and his empress Nurjehan planted chinars in Shalimar garden in Srinagar although she did not long to see its growth. During Mughal period there were about 700 gardens or more near about the Dal Lake planted by chinars.[9]

During Shahjehan's reign also the process of raising of Bune trees continued and his son Dara shukoh(whom the emperor designated as governor of northern areas) laid a garden at Bijbehara presently on main National Highway-IA. This garden/park is called Dara shikoh bagh and also Badshahi bagh. Here even today we find about 84 chinars. Among these trees there are some old tree of Dara shikuhu's time (1626 AD)and the famous tree, which has girth of 19,70 meters at ground level and 13,30 meters at breast height. Besides we find the trees of Mughal times at *Satarmoth-Khadder-moh* park (100 trees) and on Srinagar Chari Sharief road at kralpora, Wathura, Chadura and Nagam, on Srinagar kangan and Srinagar Bandipora road. Even the emperor Aurangzeb had a great love of Bune. This fact can be traced from a letter written by him to his Governor expressing regret on the devastating fire hazard of Jamia Masjid Nowhatta Srinagar and enquiring about the fate of Bune tree planted in the park of the Masjid. On recovering the information that the Bune were not damaged in the fire, he heaved a sigh of relief and remarked that the Mosque could be rebuilt in a year or two; but it will take a long long time to beautify it with Bune trees.

Introduction of Bune (Chinar) in Kashmir by Mughals however doesn't stand the test of history; because the first Mughal Emperor- Akbar, who annexed and visited the valley for the first time points out in his memories-Akbar Nama: that the king along with his 34 guards took shelter in a hollow trunk of a Bune tree when rains over took them on their journey to Srinagar. The same type of record is available in Tuzuk-jehangiri, Jahangir and his seven guards took shelter in hallow base of a chinar tree along with their horses. Thus Bune was already growing in the Kashmir valley when Mughals annexed it within their domain. The statement is also substantiated by the fact that the mystic poetess of Reshi cult the Maderre-Irfan of *Shiekh Noor-u –Din Noorani*[RA] (779H-842H--1377-1438AD). Lal Ded in her wakhs (poems) refers to a noble faithful wife to a Shehej Bune (pleasantly cool shaded bune) - which indicates that the Bune existed in the valley much before this period.

Peeping further in the past we find that there is a mention of such Boneh, Which due to their old age had turned rotten and hallow at the base and would automatically catch fire- in kalhans Rajtaragni (*By Stean 1800 AD*).Catching of fire by old hallow trees and dry branches is a fact as also observed by one Haji Zaman Mir of village Chattergam (District Budgam) some 50 years ago, as narrated by him to this writer, when he happened to be present in this village to record the measurement of a Bune growing near the mosque of Hazrat Syed Qasim Sahib[RA] in the year A.D 1986 fall. This tree turned out to be the biggest living tree of the valley and outside its habitat.

Proceeding still backwards to the pit dwellers of the valley, as found in the village Burzahama, a little distance away from the northern foreshore road of famous Dal lake and cave dwellers, i.e, Guphkrals of Tral- throws a great deal of light on the lifestyle and living conditions of these ancient people. On digging at these sites the archeologists found some charcoal at very depths. Samples obtained indicated that charcoal was prepared from some locally available bushes and trees including Maples and *populas ciliata*. Boneh wood was totally absent; this finding has been substainted by examination of pollen grains in fossil remain of temperate vegetation of this time. The Bune therefore was not found in the valley during the period of 3000-2000 BC(Singh and Kachroo, 1963 and Vishva Mitra 1966). These findings make us to assume that the Bune was introduced in the valley after 2000BC. Let us search out this probable period. As pointed out by some naturalists that the Bune does not reproduce itself naturally through seed out its natural habitat, hence this tree has not propagated outside through, by wind, water, birds and or animals. It is the man who is responsible for its existence in the central Asia, Afghanistan, Iran, North-western Pakistan and

Northern India. The Greeks and Romans introduced Bune on a large scale in Europe in order to manufacture ornamental doors and windows and fancy furniture. Thus it is most probable that this tree may have been brought to Kashmir from some of the cities of central Asia, which may be linked with Kashmir, with the trade relations or cultural activities. The history records that the Kashmiri were having good relations with the inhabitants of the cities of Khotan, Khucha etc of Central Asia and some had taken to reside permanently in these cities. They were intelligent enough to learn the art and science of raising this Bune (*Bamzai 1980*).

The most probable period of its introduction in Kashmir is however presumed to be the time. When Buddhism was introduced in Kashmir, probably before or during the period of Ashoka, the ruler of Magada (271-231BC).(*Kalhans Rajtrangni and Bagwan Buddha by Dhramanand Kosambi*). Ashoka's kingdom flanked from east of Hindukush to Bengal. After annexing Kashmir, the emperor visited the valley and laid the foundation of a city named as Puranadhisthena (*Present pandrethan*) and gifted a Bodhasanga along with 5000 Budh monks; constructed cachnyas and vihars- thus making the city a sect of great learning and centre for spread of Buddhism. The important requirements for prayers and meditation (Dhatus) in Buddhism are "Holy Rivers, nallahs, springs" etc.(Caltyas). While all other requirements could be met with ease in the valley, but they could not find a tree resemble the Bodhi tree that is *Ficus religiosa* which has got great eminence in the Buddhism.

After a thorough search the Greek Buddhist Monk Daramaraksita who was responsible for spread of Buddhism in central Asia with active support of Buddhist king Mahendra (*Bapet 1950*), came to conclude that the Bune (plane tree) has the required characteristics of a Bodhi tree because:

1. The plane tree is the tallest and much thicker in girth among the broad leaved trees found in J&K, with mighty spreading crown, thick long branches and broad palmate leaves, thus providing cool shade in hot season and intercepting rainfall.
2. The tree can survive for a very long time and in case it may fall down naturally or die due to old age, it is capable of producing sufficient epocromic branches all around its base to grow into anew tree.
3. The tree can be reproduced by seed or by branch cuttings (preferably epicormic branches with a portion of wood attached to the branch) with ease.

As a result the epicromic and other green branches and rooted cuttings in containers were brought to the valley by kashmiri Buddhists from the cities of Greece and central Asia who travelled with Dharmaksita and planted them near the Buddhists sites of learning. HeunTsang and Ooking in their travelogues have given some insights of this exodous of people from central Asia. The tree was given protection, respect and was considered as holy tree, neither to be cut nor to be used for any purpose. Even the use of dry branches as firewood was prohibited. They named it the Buddhi tree (tree of Buddha), which on passage of time transformed to Bune tree or simply to Bune. These men of letters also taught the locals of valley the art of sculpture designing. This art is even today visible as engraved on stones, clay models and intricate carvings on Kashmir handicrafts. The introduction of Ginko biloba as a Buddhist (meditation) tree in China and Japan by Buddhist monks. This tree is found in Chankiang province at Changue-Hsien with in an area of 26 sq kilometers due to protection given to it by Buddhist monks. Thus we may conclude that the Bune *(plantus-orientalis linns)* was introduced in Kashmir sometimes between 300BC to100AD.Bune being considered as an alternative to the Buddhi tree has mentioned by Sir Aurel Stein in his commentary Rajtharangi(waves of kings) 1800AD, where he mentions of the confluence of sindh nalla with jehlum river at Shadipora. He writes, "A small island of solid masonary rises in the river bed at the confluence point of two river jehlum and Sind." This (place) is an object of regular pilgrimages of particular parvans throughout the year. On it (island)stands an old Bune tree which to the pious Kashmirian represents the far famed Ficus religiosa tree of real Prayaga.[10]

Nishat Bagh would be a garden of pleasure. Chinar tree is a native of Greece and Western Asia. Both Romans and Greeks love it because of its shade. *(Britannica encyclopedia)*. Chinars on Ropa Lank, Sona Lank (Char chinar) were planted during Afghan period. Moghal emperors decorated the garden outside the temple of Mattan with beautiful chinars. Its girth can be more than 63` as found at Bijbehara. Manashal and Bhagi Safa rongly called Baghi Joroka were decorated by Chinar tree by Nur jehan empress are still extant.

In the civil lines near Tourist Reception Centre great Chinars have been spoiled by removing the first layer of its trunk which have resulted its decay. It is a royal tree and like the Wanjut belongs to the state. It attains its magnificent size. In their old age the Chinars decay and many trees at Nasim bagh and Bijbehara are hallowed on.[11]

The tree of Gardens and Parks.

If you happen to visit the famous gardens of Nishat or Shalimar, Nagin or Naseem, Kokernag or Achabal or the parks of Verinag or Bijbehara, Polo ground or Sher-i-Kashmir, Nehru Park or Dal view, Char

Chinari or Poshwari, you will definetly come across a wonderful, majestic and graceful tree called Bune in Kashmir Language. This massive tree with wide stout spreading crown, thick palm, Shaped floral leaves, changing their colour with onset of seasons, add to the natural beauty of this value of love and romance, this vale of paradise and it is due to this season that all of us are emotionally attached to this tree and have chosen it to be the symbol of the state's grandeur and good will. May it be a delicately designed shawl or Shahtoosh, Carpet or Crewel, a wood carving or a papier mashie; the label of Bune is guaranteed designation of its purity and superior quality. It is our prized proud heritage.[12]

The Biggest and the Oldest Bune.

The Bune attains large dimensions and a long life under favourable conditions as obtained in Kashmir valley. Baderwah and Kishtwar, especially on the alluvial deposits of river Jhelum and Sindhnallah in Kashmir valley and Neru Nallah in Baderwah. Its rate of growth is slow during first five years and then it increases regularly upto an age of 250 years. After about 350 years the increment percentage decreases and it is only the comparatively younger branches, which put on the increment in girth and length.

The average yearly diameter increment as per above data is 0.0148mts. It may be noted that the above growth data has been calculated for a few trees growing on a comparatively better soil and environmental conditions in Kashmir valley. In case the growth conditions are not favourable than we may expect the yearly increment growth to the extent of 40 to 50% of the above referred data. The maximum height attained by the Bune may go upto 50 to 55mts in favourable conditions. In his book "Silviculture of Indian trees " (vol.iii,page 893) Troup records that Mr. Macdonall in A.D.1903 recorded the girth of two large trees one at Dragmullah (District Kupwars) having a girth of 50 feet(that is 15 meter) and second at jhama with a girth of 43 feet (12.90 meters). These two trees do not exist at present. The largest recorded girth by Dr. Stewart at Srinagar was 28 feet (8.40 meters).

Brandis mentions that the *Nasim Bagh* on the border of the Dal lake (Great Kashmir lake) is a large grove of plane trees planted by Akbar soon after he had taken Kashmir in 1586. In 1838 Vigne found the average girth of these trees to be 13ft, and supposed their age to be 248 years. The largest, close to the water,close to the water, average 20ft. Of two trees 170 years old at Brien in Kashmir, Vigne found one 16 ft.,2 inch., the other 20ft, 10 inch in girth.

Sir Walter Lawrence writes in his book *"valley of Kashmir"* that the Langer Bune in Chinar Bagh (Srinagar) is the finest specimen of the Bune. One old Bune he measured in Lolab (District Kupwara) was 65`-5` (20 meter) in girth at 5feet (1.53 meter)height from ground level. The age of the Bune planted in Darashikoh Park by Darashikoh (whom his father appointed as governor of northern areas in 1634 AD) after completion of park formation in the year 1636 AD will be 365 years in the year 2001 AD. The girth of hither to Kashmir's biggest bune in this park as recorded by Fotedar A.N (*in the journal of Ecc tax: Bot: vol.ii, 1987*) is 19.7 meters at ground level and13.30 meters at breast height. This Bune is now broken at the height of 5 meters where from it has produced 5 new branches. Now it is in the state of decay and death.[13]

REFERENCES

1. Wadoo, M.S., *"Trees Of Our Heritage"* Idris-Pub. Kashmir, 2008.
2. Raina, A.K., *"Tourism Industry In Kashmir"* Shipra Pub. Delhi, 2002.
3. Farid, Syed Ajaz., *"Tourism In Kashmir"* New Delhi, 2003.
4. O'CONNER V.C.Scott., *"The Charms Of Kashmir"* New Delhi, 1992.
5. Paltoo, Riaz. A., *"Kashmir Speaks"* Lal Bazar Srinagar, 2007.
6. Vidyarthi, O.P. Sharma IFS., *"Plants Of Parks And Gardens"* Jammu,2003.
7. Brooke's John. *"Gardens Of Paradise: The history and design of great Islamic gardens"* London, 1987.
8. Stuart C.M.Villers., *"Gardens Of Great Mughals"* Cosmo publisher, Delhi.
9. Bakshi. S. R., *"Kashmir, Tourism, Monuments and folklore"* New Delhi, 1997.
10. Das. S. N., *"Kashmir"* Book centre Srinagar, 2008.
11. Norris Dermot., *"Kashmir The Switzerland of India"* Gowkadal Srinagar, 1989.
12. Mattoo Ab Majid.,*"Kashmir Under The Mughals"* Srinagar, 1988.
13. Majid Gulshan., *"Gardens Of Mughal India: a history and guide"*Srinagar, 2006.
14. Fazil Abul., *"Akbar Nama"* Bib, Ind. Calcutta, 1897-1939.
15. Brown Percy. *"Chinar Leaves"* Spink Calcutta.
16. Brown Percy., *"India's Architecture (Islamic Period)"*London, 1942.
17. Gervis, P., *"This Is Kashmir"* London, 1954.
18. Jahangir Emperor., *"Tuzuk-i-Jahangiri"* By A.Rogers, London,1909-14.
19. Hassan B, Ali Kashmiri.,*"Tawarik-i-Kashmiri"* Bodlecan 315.
20. Lawrence, W.R.,*"The Valley Of Kashmir"* London, 1895.
21. NEVE, ERNEST. F., *"Beyond-The Pirpanjal"* Srinagar, 2003.
22. Bakshi, S.R., *"History of Economic Development in Kashmir"*Srinagar, 2002.

CHAPTER- VII

UNDERSTANDING THE DRAINAGE PATTERN IN URBAN INDIA

A CASE STUDY OF SRINAGAR CITY IN JAMMU AND KASHMIR

SHAHID SHAFI ITOO

INTRODUCTION

Environment is the source of life on earth and it not only directs but also determines the existence, growth and development of mankind and all its activities. Primitive man ate wild fruits- hunted and fished- all relied heavily on nature for his very existence. Even these basic activities damaged nature to some extent. At that time, man did not concern himself with conservation methods, in other words there was no need for its management because nature was able to cope with whatever damage was inflicted, quickly restoring its resources.

Of the many essential elements for the existence of human beings and animals and universally known such as air, water, food, shelter etc. water importance is rated as the highest. It is the water which gave origin to the life on this blue planet-the earth. Hence, water is considered absolutely essential to sustain life. Also the protoplasm of many living cells contains about 85% water and any substantial reduction in this level is disastrous. Furthermore, most of the bio-chemical reactions which occurs in metabolism and growth of living cells involve the medium of water. As such, water is referred as the universal solvent.

Globally, three fourth ($3/4^{th}$) of the earth's surface is covered by water. Inspite of this apparent abundance of water, less than 1% is available for human use in the form of surface waters, as 97% is contained in oceans, etc. and 2% is locked up in ice caps and glaciers. Therefore it is this less than 1% of the total Global water which is extensively exploited by man for a variety of purposes which include drinking, bathing, washing, laundering, heating and air-conditioning, irrigation, industrial processes, power generation, waste disposal and recreational purposes. In fact, every activity of man involves some use of water.

Further, as water is often drawn from springs, rivers which gave rise to site for human habitation and settlement, as such water has a political significance also. Societies developed as time passed away. Man's impact on environment grew in scope and strength beyond the optimum levels which not only resulted in the deterioration of the quality of environment but the very existence of environment. At this point, man realized the need to preserve and improve his environment. This is now shown as the ecological approach of management. Finally as a move towards this approach, Environmental Science, a recently introduced subject provides an effective approach towards the understanding of the environment of our planet, the impact of human activities on it and suggests the possible remedial measures for the same.

Consumption of Water and Disposal of Waste Water and Night Soil

The total water consumed by the whole communities in the both areas of study and the disposal options carried out for the disposal waste water and night soil, were evaluated by means of direct questionnaire method. A precisely worded questionnaire (Annexure l) pertaining to the determining factors for the evaluation of the consumption of water and disposal options was developed. By giving adequate representation to demographic setup of the concerned community, questionnaire was provided to the respondents and explained onsite. The information was collected from 30% of the total households in both study areas and conclusions drawn accordingly.

ANALYSIS AND FINDINGS

In Srinagar city, there were 30 municipal wards functioning under central Srinagar Municipal Corporation (SMC). _Their number has now risen to 68 due to addition of more colonies (Master Plan, 2000 ~ 2021). Srinagar city is by and large a plain area characterized by habitations on both sides of River Jhelum. Earlier Nalla Mar channel was used for the purpose of drainage. Later on it was filled up which called for the establishment of Urban Environment Engineering Department (UEED) to cater to the needs of drainage and sewerage system of the city. About 89 major schemes, 74 dewatering stations comprising 1500 *mohallas* have been identified for coverage of zones set up by UEED. Out of the target of 30000 meters of sewer lines, 23413 meters lines have been constructed (UEED, 2006). However these attempts seems not environmentally feasible because the existing network of sewerage and drainage was found directly affecting water bodies suchas river Jhelum, Doodganga stream, Nallah Amir Khan, Dal lake, Khushalsar lakeand Anchar lake. Furthermore, no separate storm water drainage system exist in Srinagar city. Whole sullage, storm water and other waste is carried through a system of open drains, deep drains and sewers into the water bodies without any treatment (Anonymous, 2006).

Drainage Pattern

Issues and Problems in the Sociology of Jammu & Kashmir

A thorough comparative study of drainage channels present in both areas of the study revealed the following:

A. The drainage pattern observed at Athwajan (Fig. 1) was conferred to follow *"rectangular drainage pattern"*. In this pattern of drainage system, the drainage channels join the major river (river Jhelum) almost at right angles characterized by the widely spaced drains which bring about the waste water from the whole area of Athwajan. Lateral drains were found to form a network finally joining the main drain along the National Highway Road side which in turn discharged its effluents directly into the river Jhelum. This pattern of drainage channels was observed to be suitable as per the climatic conditions (rainfall), topography, soil characteristics etc. of Athwajan area. The drainage pattern observed at Zaina Kadal (Fig. 2) was concluded to be *"parallel drainage pattern"*. This pattern of drainage channels was characterized by the separate drainage channels for each sub area (called Mohalla) running parallel to each other, finally conveying their discharge directly into the main drainage basin (River Jhelum) all along both banks of river Jhelum. Best suited for the centrally sloping topography of the Zaina Kadal area, parallel drainage pattern collects both storm Water and wastewater (through open drains) and night soil (through deep drains) and conveying directly into the river Jhelum Without any prior treatment.

Sewerage System

The sewerage system constitute overall design and layout of drains (sewers) made artificially of concrete material meant for conveying the sewage (generated from the households) for its site of disposal.

The sewerage system at site-I (Athwajan) was observed to have almost "separate sewerage system". Since about 75% of households were equipped with septic tanks for the disposal of night soil, the waste Water and storm water was found to be drained off through the open sewers.

Comparative to the site-I, site-II (Zaina Kadal) was observed to have "combined sewerage system" where both night soil (using country type latrine) as well as waste water were directly conveyed into the river Jhelum without any treatment This is because only 12-15% of households in Zaina Kadal area found to have septic disposal for night soil.

Discharge (Q) of waste water per household/ day and per person/ day at Athawajan & Zaina Kadal

As depleted by the above figures the discharge of waste water calculated from site-I resulted in a total discharge of 0 00096 cumecs (82944 liters per day) Thus each person in Athwajan area contributed a total of 48 36 11tres of waste water per day to the total discharge. As against this a total discharge of 0.0052 cumecs (449280 liters per day) was calculated from the site-II thereby Showing 64.71 liters of waste water contribution per person per day.

This relative variation of 16.35 liters per person per day between the two study areas may be attributed to the following reasons

a) More consumption of water in Zama Kadal (420 liters per household per day) as compared with Athwajan (365 liters per household per day.

b) More congestion of houses in the limited areas of Zaina Kadal (1010houses in 21.2 ha.) as compared with Athwajan (350 houses in 92 ha.)

c) Septic disposal of major portion of the Waste water generated in households of Athwajan area (70% septic tanks) as compared with Zaina Kadal (15% septic disposal).

Storm Water Quantification

Rainfall or rain that falls over the surface of the ground, a part of which is lost through evaporation in the air or percolation into the soil, constitutes the storm water. The amount of storm water reaching sewers in a combined system is usually more than the dry weather flow (Without the rainfall) as such it greatly influence the design of combined sewers.

Table 3 showing storm water quantification at two sites

S. No.	Sites	Discharge (in cumecs)
01	Athwajan	0.918
02	Zaina Kadal	0.490

The figure shown above reveals that the storm water calculated in case of site-l was relatively more (0.9l8 cumecs) than at site-II (O.490cumecs). This can be particularly attributed to the topographical and climatic differences between the two study areas. The following reasons appeared to be responsible:

1. Athwajan area being located in the lap of Zabarwan hills receives more rains than Zaina Kadal.
2. The study area in Athwaj an (92 ha.) was more than Zaina Kadal (21.2ha).
3. The storm water calculated in Athwajan area also included the runoff from the Zabarwan hills, hence adding more to the total storm water in the area.

Disposal of waste water/night soil

The disposal of waste water and night soil generated in the households needs immense care and proper disposal methods. However the disposal methods carried out in the two areas of study showed a marked different approach.

Table 6 Disposal of night soil at Athwajan and Zaina Kadal

S. No.	Sites	Method of night soil disposal	
		Septic tank	Country type
01	Athwajan	75.00	25.00
02	Zaina Kadal	20.00	80.00

About 70-73% of the households in Athwajan area were observed to dispose off their night soil separately by means of attached Septic tanks. These septic tanks were actually the soakage pits used for the final disposal of sewage (night soil mainly) and mostly found in newly constructed houses which have attached such facility well before hand while constructing the house. On the other hand, Zaina Kadal area using combined sewerage system mainly relied on country type of latrines for the disposal of night soil and other wastes (85% country type disposal). These country type latrines were attached to old houses without septic tanks rather disposing their wastes through surface drains which finally entered the main natural drainage channel (river Jhelum) in the Zaina Kadal area. In nutshell, Athwajan area was dominated by septic disposal of night soil while in Zaina Kadal country type latrine disposal dominated.

SUGGESTIONS

The study revealed that 85% of households in Zaina Kadal and above 20% households in Athwajan completely relied on country type of latrine system using large volumes of water for its convenience through open drainage channels. These drainage channels have poor connectivity and often get chocked in rainy season resulting in flooding of streets and roads (especially in Athwajan). Furthermore, the predominance of open surface drains in the inner wards of residential areas of the Whole Srinagar city in general and in study areas in particular, were found to degrade the urban environmental quality rendering them vulnerable to many unhygienic conditions and health hazards.

In addition to the above mentioned facts these open drains ultimately disposed off into the main natural drainage basin (River Jhelum) without any treatment in both areas, thereby enhancing the levels of water pollution of this fragile water ecosystem, the life line of Kashmir valley. Based on the present analytical study, drastic overhauling of sewerage and drainage disposal system in whole Srinagar city is suggested Moreover; there is a

Issues and Problems in the Sociology of Jammu & Kashmir

need for the comprehensive planning of drainage systems and establishment of subsequent treatment plants for the waste effluents prior to their disposal. This not only will ensure the overall better quality of urban environment in Srinagar city but also will reduce the existing levels of pollution of major water bodies like Jhelum. Positive contribution from the associated departments like Srinagar Municipal Corporation (SMC), Urban Environment Engineering Department (UEED), Srinagar Development Authority (SDA), etc, is the need of the hour. Continuous environmental monitoring of the drainage systems with an integrated scientific approach for the disposal of waste Waters will not only enhance the proper sanitation of the region but also improve the quality of life. This will probably ensure our longer sustenance.

REFERENCES

Anonymous, 2006. *Draft Sewerage* and *Drainage Master Plan, Srinagar City.* Operational Research Bureau, J&K.

Burkhard, R., Deletic, A. and Craig. A. 2000. Techniques for water and waste water management: A *review of techniques and their integration in planning, urban water,* 2:1197-221.

Clerk, R., Parkins, A. and wood, S. E. 1997. Water sustainability in urban areas-an Adelaide and region case study. Report one - an exploration of the concept. *Department of Environment and Natural Resources,* Adelaide, Australia. Draft.

David, H. F., Lipta'k, B.G. and Bouis, P.A. 1996. Environmental Engineer's *Handbook,* Lewis Publications, New York.

Duggal, K. N. 1998. Elements of Environmental Engineering S. Chand and Company Ltd, New Delhi.

Galuzzi, MR. and Pflam, J. M. 1996. Integrating drainage, water quality, wetlands and habitat in a planner community development, ASCE. *Journal of Urban Planning and Development,* 122 (3)1101 - 108.

Haeney, T.P., Pitt, R. and Field, R. 1999. Innovative urban wet weather flow management systems. U.S. *Environmental Protection Agency,* Cincinnati, Ohio.EPA.600/R-99/029.

Harremoes, P. 1997 _ Integrated water and waste management Water science and *Technology,*35 (9): 11-20.

Hellstorm, D., Jeppsson, U. and Karrman, E.2000. A framework for system analysis of sustainable urban water management. *Environmental Impact Assessment Review.*20: 311-321.

Joshua, E. Y., Kennedy, C., Saiz, S. and Pressnail, K. 2005. Towards Sustainable Development; The Need to Consider Infrastructure Interactions *Can.J.* *Civ.Eng.* 32: 45-57.

Kishtwar, A. 2006. Focus on Jammu and Kashmir, Cresecent House Publications.

Kulash, W. M. 2001. Residential streets, Urban Land Institute, Washington, D. C.

Malano, H.M.2000. A drainage service approach to participatory irrigation and drainage management. Proceedings of the 8th ICD. *International Drainage Workshop,* Vol. III, New Delhi.

Master Plan 2000-2021. *Srinagar Metropolitan Area.* Srinagar Development Authority, Government Press, Srinagar.

Mitchell, V.G., Mein, R.G. and Mc.Mahon, T.A.1996. Evaluating the resource potential of storm water and waste water: An Australian Perspective. P. 9-13. *Proceedings of the 7th International Conference* on *Urban storm drainage.* Hannover, Germany, 9-13.

Pandit, A. K., Khan, A. H.(1996) Ecology Environment and Energy, Deptt. Of distance education, University of Kashmir.

Qamar, J .S. 1998. Integrated Water Resources Management Study: Appraisal of the National Water Strategy. Internal report. 98/13. Lahore, Pakistan, IWASRI.

Qureshi, A. L., Chandio, S.N. and Kori, S.N. 2000. Performance evaluation of surface drains in LBGD project area: A case study of spinal drains. *Proceedings of the National Seminar on Drainagein Pakistan*, Jamshorro, Pakistan, MUET.

Rakesh, H., Mundra, S.N. and Ram, S. 1997. *Irrigation Drainage International and National Perspectives*, Agro. Tech. Publications, Udaipur.

Rao, P. V. 2005. A Text Book of *Environmental Engineering*. Prentice Hall Pvt. Ltd., New Delhi.

Rehman, C. A. and Rafiq, A.Q. 1995. Future strategies for making drainage systems sustainable. *Proceedings of National Workshop on Drainage System Performance in the Indus Plain and Future Strategies*. Tandojam, Pakistan, DRIP.

Savindra, S. 2006. *Geomorphology*. Prayag Pustak Bhawan, Allahabad (India).

Smerdon, T., Wagget, R. and Grey, R.1997.Sustainable Housing Options for   Independent Energy, Water Supply and Sewage. BSRIA, Braknell, Berkshira, U.K.

Speir, C. and Stephenson, K. 2002. Does sprawl cost us all? Isolatinf the effects of housing patterns on public water and sewer cost. *Journal of the American Planning Association*.68 (1): 56-70.

Tarar, R. N. 1995. Drainage system in the Indus plain- An Overview. *Proceedings of   the National Workshop on Indus Plain and Future Strategies*. Tandojam, Pakistan, DRIP.

UEED, 2006. Detailed Project Report. Urban Environmental Engineering Department, J&K Government.

Walesh, S.G. and Carr, R. 1989. Urban Sulface Water Management. Wiley and Sons, New York.

Wetzal, R.G. and Likens, G.E. 2000. LimnologicalAnab/sis 3rd Edition S Riner, P E Verlag Publications, New York.

Xiao, Q., McPherson, E. G., Simpson, J.R. and Ustin, S.L.1998. Rainfal interception by sachriniento's Urban 235-244. Forest Journal of Arboriculture, 24: 235-244.

CHAPTER- VIII

WOMEN EDUCATION IN INDIA

SPECIAL REFERENCE TO JAMMU AND KASHMIR

MS. RUCHI

INTRODUCTION

"The question of the Education of children cannot be solved unless efforts are made simultaneously to solve the women's education. And I have no hesitation in saying that as long as we do not have real mother teachers who can successfully impart true education to our children they will remain uneducated even though they may be going to schools.She must have special knowledge of the management of the home, care of children, their education etc" - (M.K.Gandhi).

The status of women in the Indian society has been subjected to many great changes over the past few millennia. From equal status with men in ancient times through the low points of the medieval period, to the promotion of equal rights by many reformers, the history of women in India has been eventful. Education of women, therefore occupies top priority among various measures to improve the status of women in India.

"Truly no argument is required in defense of women's education. For my part, I have always been strongly of the opinion that while it may be possible to neglect men's education it is not possible to neglect women's education. The reasons are obvious if you educate the women, probably men will be affected thereby, and in any event children will be affected" - (Jawaharlal Nehru).

In India women education has been neglected so far. But now it has been realized that women's education is equally important as of men. The University Grants Commission has rightly remarked about it "if general education had to be limited to men or to women, then opportunity should be given to women, for then it would more surely be passed on to the next generation".

History of women education in Pre- Independence India

Women in ancient India enjoyed a very high social status. They were given educational opportunities equal to men. There was no discrimination between sexes. Brahmins girls were taught Vedic knowledge and Kshatriya girls were taught the use of sword, bow and arrow. In fact education was allowed for women not as an opportunity, but as a must. The women carried on not only learning but also teaching; that they professed teaching is understood from the word *upadhayani* by Patanjali. In Vedic period there were famous educated women such as Maitreyi, Gargi, Ghosa and Sulabha who were well versed in many fields of education.

In the post- Vedic period (after 300B.C) a drastic deterioration took place in the women position. The degradation of women lasted till the beginning of the twentieth century. Reasons might be the ruling Aryans were busy in war and for that a need for more men resulted and sons were valued. The other reason might be ancestor worship. As the men gained paramountey by virtue of the status, the women were made inferior class and degraded. A multitude of derogatory attributes were ascribed to them. They were denied access to educational opportunity. They were no more allowed to prosecute Vedic studies. Due to the absence of education, the women were deceived to be fit for nothing. Since the girls were not educated, early marriages became common. The *purdah* also came into royal families. *Sati- daho* was also revived. Thus women were burdened with cumulative injustices and subjected to gross discrimination in all spheres (Desai, Mazumdar, Bhansali in Jain and Rajput [ed] 2003).

In the early decades of the nineteenth century, women were almost completely excluded from the formal system of education and it was believed that girls could acquire all that was necessary, as education, in their domestic surroundings (Desai 1977). It was a period of deep rooted prejudice against women's education, encapsulated in such homilies as 'educate a girl and you give a knife into her hands', and 'education will entail widowhood upon a girl'. It is therefore not surprising to find that when the government of Bombay undertook an inquiry into the condition of indigenous education in the 1820's the district reports did not record even a single instance of girls attending school in the province. The earliest efforts to educate girls were made by Christian missionaries. In the city of Bombay the first school girls was started in 1824. Most of the girls attending this school were Christians (Ibid).

However, a great pioneer was the Mahatma Jyotiba Phule himself a lower caste who, with his wife Savitribai in 1848, opened the first school for shudra and atishudra girls in western India. Phule held the view that the low status of shudras was due to the denial of education to them. He believed in imparting education to women as a matter of justice in itself. Savitribai said, 'Education alone can banish ignorance and inhuman behavior and make us human beings'. Those who were able to obtain higher education were mostly from the upper castes, thus underscoring the link between access to education, class and gender.

Issues and Problems in the Sociology of Jammu & Kashmir

During the period 1922-1947 the enrolment of girls in primary schools moved up from nearly 35 lakhs in 1946-47 and enrolment in secondary schools increased from about 37 thousands in 1921-22 to a record of 281 thousands. But significant progress occurred in higher education where the enrolment of girls increased from merely 1529 in 1921-22 to as high as 23,207 in 1947. In spite of all this expansion, the enrolment of girls was only 2.4 percent of their population.

Table- 2.1

Women and girls literacy rates in Pre- Independence Period

Year	Percentage of Literacy	Primary School	Middle School	Secondary School	University and Colleges	Others	Total
1881 -82	0.2	124491	*	2054	6	5151	2066
1901 -02	0.7	345397	34386	103309	264	2812	393168
1921 -22	1.8	1198550	92466	36698	1529	11599	1340842
1946 -47	6.0	3475165	321508	280772	23207	56090	4156742

Source: Quinquennial Report –Ministry of Education and Culture

Women Education in Post-Independence Period

With the overall aim in the Post-independence period to show concern and to work towards the expansion of women's education, a look at plan documents, as well as the reports of various Committees and Commissions indicate that there has not been evolved even a uniform view that there should be the same curricula for boys and girls (John1992:28-30). After independence the first step was the establishment of the University Education Commission (1948-49) which made certain recommendations regarding women's education. But the most important development in the field of women's education after independence was the setting up of a National Committee for Women's Education in 1958 under the Chairpersonship of Smt. Durgabai Deshmukh.

The Union Ministry of Education set up the National Council for Women's Education in 1959. Most of the state governments have also established state councils for women's education. Smt. Hansa Mehta Committee was appointed in 1961 by the National Council for Women's Education to examine the problem of curricula for girls at all stages of education. Another Committee was appointed by the Council in May 1965 with Shri.

Issues and Problems in the Sociology of Jammu & Kashmir

M. Bhaktavatsalan as the Chairman to look into the girl's education. The Education Commission (1964-66) also made valuable recommendations regarding women's education in India. The National Committee (1974) studied various aspects of the status of women and their education. More recently the National Policy on Education (1986) recommended in clearer terms free education for girls up to the secondary school stage.

Progress since Independence - a situational analysis

Literacy

During the present century, the country has made spectacular progress in promoting the interests of women. The literacy rate went up from about 7 percent in 1901 to 8.86 percent in 1951, 15.35 percent in 1961, 21.97 percent in 1971, 29.76 percent in 1981, 39.29 percent in 1991, 53.67 percent in 2001 and 65.46 percent in 2011. But there is still a wide gap in male and female literacy. This is obvious from the following table:

Table- 2.2
Literacy Rate in India (Percent) : 1951-2011

Census Year	Persons	Male	Female	Male-Female gap in literacy rate
1951	18.33	27.16	8.86	18.30
1961	28.3	40.4	15.35	25.15
1971	34.45	45.96	21.97	23.98
1981	43.57	56.38	29.76	26.62
1991	52.21	64.13	39.29	24.84
2001	64.83	75.26	53.67	21.59
2011	74.04	82.14	65.46	16.68

Source: Census of India 2011(the 1981 literacy rates excludes Assam where the 1981 census could not be conducted, the 1991 census Literacy rates excludes Jammu and Kashmir).

The study of the importance and impediments of girl's education showed that in our country the education of girls is lagging behind that of boys. Illiteracy of parents, especially of mothers had always been a hindrance in the spread of girls' education. Besides this, economic impediments (physical facilities, teachers, curriculum, wastage and stagnation) also added to the non- enrolment of girls. About 80 percent girls dropped out by the time they reached class 8th because in India, it is generally considered that schooling of girls is a loss of time and earning to the family (Mishra, 1991).

Issues and Problems in the Sociology of Jammu & Kashmir

Recent years, of course, have witnessed a change in this context of male-female differential in literacy even in traditional societies. There has been an evident decline in the male- female differential in literacy as the female literacy rates have increased more rapidly than the male literacy rates. This may be attributed to a very low base of female literacy and also to the opening up of large number of schools in the rural areas. Consequently, the number of female teachers has also increased considerably which has had a catalytic effect upon the process of dissemination of female education. Moreover the increasing social awakening and increasing male literacy have stimulated female literacy, as the female literacy is now becoming matrimonial precondition (Ibid).

Literacy and education had also changed attitudes towards child marriage. There is also some impact of women's educational level and their participation in various economic activities in their age at marriage. In Bhadra's study (1999), data indicate that among the illiterate females the mean age at marriage in case of both rural and urban is at least five years lower than the females with graduate and above educational background. It is noticed that the mean age at marriage of Indian girls increases with their education and changing outlook. Such change in age at marriage is always related to the enhanced status of women in Indian society. This study has also attempted to look into the relationship between age at marriage and education among the Scheduled Caste women of village Chohala.

During the decade 1981-91 there has been a steady increase in the age at marriage for girls from 15.5 years in 1981 to 19.5 years in 1991. There has been a marked improvement in the female child's participation in education. On the whole, enrolment of girls in school has increased eight-fold from 5.4 million in 1950-51 to 44.9 million in 1992-93; the school enrolment at primary stage was above hundred in many states. The vast increase in school enrolment at the higher level indicated a significant improvement in girl's education (Bhadra, 1999).

While there has been some catching up in the literacy rates for males and females between rural and urban areas, the gender gap continue to be unacceptably large, especially for females. Only 46.70% of females in rural areas were literate as opposed to nearly 73.20 percent females in urban areas in 2001(Census 2001). Though there has been substantial increase in literacy rates in both urban and rural areas, the gap between the two sectors has not narrowed appreciably. As with India, many states have large rural- urban differentials in female literacy. In Bihar and Jharkhand less than 30 percent rural women were literate in 2001, whereas their counterparts in urban areas had a literacy rate of 62.59% and 69.96% respectively. A major problem facing Indian education system, especially in rural areas, is that although the students may enroll at the beginning, many of them do not complete their schooling especially the girl students.

Table- 2.3
Rural-Urban Literacy in India (Percent):1991-2001

Census Year	1991			2001		
Population	Male	Female	Total	Male	Female	Total
Rural	57.90	30.60	44.7	71.40	46.70	59.40
Urban	81.10	64.00	73.1	86.70	73.20	80.30
Total	64.13	39.29	52.2	75.83	54.16	65.38

Source: Abstracts, Selected Educational Statistics (2005-2006), Government of India, Ministry of Human Resource Development, department of Higher Education.

Increasing access to higher education is associated with increasing gender parity- something like 10 percent of women enrolment in higher education in 1950-51 to 40.4 percent in 2006-07. Faculty wise disparity is however, glaring. Women's enrolment is as high as 51percent in Arts but as low as 20 percent in Science, 4 percent in Engineering and 3.6 percent in Medicine. Hence, for professional courses scenario needs to be drastically improved (Bhushan, 2006).

An important study (Afzal and Ahmad, 2008) concludes that during the first five years of the 21st century, 20 percent more men students were enrolled as compared to women students. The data with respect to faculty-wise enrolment shows that there was a big gender gap in the enrolment in various faculties of higher education-10 percent in the Faculty of Arts; 20 percent in the Faculty of Science; 27 percent in the Faculty of Commerce/Management; 56 percent in the Faculty of Engineering/Technology; nine percent in the Faculty of Medicine; 65 percent in the Faculty of Agriculture; 55 percent in the Faculty of Veterinary Science; 59 percent in Faculty of Law. Only the faculty of education had 3 percent more enrolment of women students than men students.

Mandal (1980) observed that the great discrimination prevails regarding education in girls in Bihar. According to him there is a great apathy towards girl's education because the people think that if their daughters get education they will be in trouble in finding out suitable marriage partners. So education is a curse for their fathers. Women education at the both University –College levels has been diversified and reoriented in tune with the changing requirements of society, industry and trade. The number of women enrolled in institutions of higher education increased from 40,000 in

Issues and Problems in the Sociology of Jammu & Kashmir

1950-51 to about 14, 37,000 in 1990-91 recording an increase of more than 36 times over the forty-year period. And in the year 2004-05 the number increased to 3,971,407. Proportion of women entering higher education 1950-51 was 10.9 percent and in 2002-03 it was 40.04 percent. The number of women per 100 men in 1950-51 was 14 which increased to 67in 2002-03.

There are also wide disparities in enrolment by region, caste and tribe and by gender. These differences impact on women from the disadvantaged groups. In 2001-02, the proportions of SC/ST students were as follows: Scheduled castes 11.5 percent (1,016,182) SC men 8 percent (7, 06,769) and SC women 3.5 percent (309,813). In M.Phil/ Ph.D. programs, there were 53119 students all over the country. Of these 36.3 percent (19,299) were women, 5.9 percent (3,133) SC students. There were about 824 SC women i.e. 4.3 percent of all women research students. It is quite well known that in spite of a very well formulated policy of positive discrimination, the representation of SC students is not adequate and the proportion of women is negligible. They generally join general education courses and are denied access to elite courses and institutions (Chanana 1998).

Disciplinary choices are affected by socio-economic factors especially in the case of Scheduled caste students whose representation remains marginal in higher education. But they too, are better represented in states in which women have better representation and in which higher education facilities have expanded in recent years. The relationship between availability of disciplinary choices and women's ability to access them are not directly related, nor are they dependent on women's academic achievement. The reasons cited for this are mainly due to social ethics. Large majority of women may be deprived of exercising free options in selecting subjects of their choice in school, as in case of girls, parents generally take decision regarding the academic stream to be pursued. This decision is guided by the consideration that girls are not expected to earn work or earn before marriage and education is only an investment to fall back upon in case of the daughter becoming a widow or being deserted.

Women Education in Jammu and Kashmir

In the National Educational Scenario, J&K state is subsumed as educationally backward in reference to the established indices namely literacy rate, teacher pupil ratio, dropout rate and the absorption pattern of the educated persons. The disquieting features are low literacy rate, higher drop-out rate, gender disparity, mismatch between education and employment. The J&K State strictly adheres to the National Education Policy and with the exponential growth of the institutional framework and reach of services as a consequence of sustained investment folio through plan strategy; improvement in every parameter is visible. The improvement is more pronounced in the field of girls' literacy. Education is one of the most valuable means in achieving gender equality and empowerment of women (Suri, 1999).

Education of women is an effective tool for women's empowerment not only from the point of view of literacy, but has inter-linkage with other social parameters i.e. population growth, health care, education of children etc. It enables rural women to acquire new knowledge and technology, required for improving and developing their tasks in all fields. Female education is essential for higher standards of health and improved 'maternal competence' which leads to lower infant mortality. It also raises women's economic productivity (Ibid).

Women constitute about 47 percent of the total population in J&K. Women development, no doubt, has been part of the development planning in the state since the inception of Five Year Plans but the shift in approach from welfare to the development of women took place in the Sixth Plan onwards. But despite so many positive outcomes in the successive Plans and the progress made over the past 60 years, female literacy has remained very low in J&K state as compared to male literacy. Gender disparity in literacy in J&K is a historical phenomenon.

Women Education after Independence in J&K

Literacy is an effective instrument for social and economic development and national integration. It is defined in census operations as the ability to read and write with understanding in many languages. In modern context, the word refers to reading and writing at a level adequate for communication or at level that let some understand and communicate ideas in a literate society, so as to take part in that society. The United Nations Educational, Scientific and Cultural organisation (UNESCO) defined literacy as *'the ability to identify, understand, interpret, create, communicate and compute, using printed and written materials associated with varying contexts. Literacy involves a continuum of learning to enable an individual to achieve his or her goals, to develop his or her knowledge and potential and to participate fully in the society'* (IMPA, 2008). Over the years, the females' literacy rate in J&K has increased though not in the same way as that of males. According to the census of 2001 in Jammu and Kashmir, literacy level is 54.46 percent. The state ranked 33rd amongst the 35 odd states and union territories of India.

Within the state, the spatial variations in literacy are quite wide. The gap between the highest (Jammu, 77 percent) and lowest (Badgam, 42.5 percent) literacy districts for instance, is almost 25 percent. Only 6 districts out of a total of 14 have literacy rate higher than the state average figure the remaining 8 have almost two-fifths of their population without the ability to read and write (Census, 2001). These educationally, most backward districts viz. Kupwara, Baramula, Pulwama, Anantnag, and Badgam in the valley and Doda, Udhampur and Punch in Jammu province form a contiguous belt in middle of the state covering the mountainous and forested region which separates two clusters of high literacy rates- one in south and the south-west comprising Jammu, Rajouri and Kathua and the other in the north-east comprising Srinagar, Kargil and Leh.

It is a well-known facts that about 80 percent of the people in Jammu and Kashmir live in rural areas, where the educational facilities beyond the mixed primary schools are hardly sufficient.

Table-2.8

Percentage of Male- Female Literacy in Total/Rural/Urban Population in 1981 and 2001

Total/ rural/urban	Persons		Males		Females	
	1981	2001	1981	2001	1981	2001
Total	30.64	54.46	41.46	65.75	18.37	41.82
Rural	25.01	48.22	36.35	60.34	12.19	35.09
Urban	51.12	72.12	59.87	80.30	41.05	62.22

Source: 2001 census

Rural-Urban differentials in literacy are also wide. The above Table reveals that educational development has remained urban-centric both among males and females in the state. The literacy rate for rural areas is 48.22percentagainst 72.17 percent for urban areas according to 2001 census. Again female literacy in rural areas at 35.09 percent is very low and is less than half of the literacy in urban areas.

According to the latest census conducted in 2011 there is about 9 percent increase in the overall literacy rate in Jammu and Kashmir with Jammu District leading the way with 77.02 percent. The total literacy rate registered in the state was 68.74 percent (males-78.26 percent and females-58.01 percent) compared to 54.46 percent in 2001. While the literacy rate in urban areas shot up to 78.19 percent compared to 72.12 percent in 2001, rural areas, because of lack of infrastructure, were lagging much behind. According to the census, rural literacy has touched 64.97 percent.

Issues and Problems in the Sociology of Jammu & Kashmir

Table-2.9

Percentage of Male-Female Literacy in Total/Rural/ Urban population 2011

Total/rural/urban	Persons	Males	Females
Total	68.74	78.26	58.01
Rural	64.97	75.51	53.36
Urban	78.19	84.90	70.19

Source: 2011 census

The Table above shows that there exists a huge gap in rural-urban female literacy rate in the state and also the gender gap in the literacy according to the census 2011 is 20.25.

Out of the total 200 blocks in the state 109 blocks are identified as educationally backward blocks in Jammu and Kashmir. Rural literacy rate of J&K is 42.93 percent (2001) which is below the national average. In respect of female literacy rate, it is less than national average and Gender gap is higher than national average in 109 blocks. Besides, ST female literacy rate is below 10 percent in 62 predominant ST blocks (as per 1991 census). The SC female literacy rate is below 10 percent in 34 predominant SC blocks (1991 census). This shows clear gender disparity. Besides, girl's participation in enrolment and retention at upper primary level from the disadvantaged groups and caste that of SC&ST is a big challenge.

Table-2.10

Sex- wise Literacy rate in Total/Rural/Urban population by Tehsil/Block R.S Pura: 1981 and 2001

Total/rural/urban	Persons		Males		Females	
	1981	2001	1981	2001	1981	2001
Total	42.01	76.1	52.52	83.9	31.75	67.6
Rural	41.82	75.7	51.76	83.6	31.07	67.3
Urban	52.26	80.5	61.02	87.2	40.97	71.5

Source: Census 2001

The above Table shows the sex wise literacy of both the rural and urban population of R.S Pura block. There exists a huge gap in the male –female literacy of both rural and urban areas, while there is an increase in the literacy rate in total from 42.01 percent in 1981 to 76.1 percent in 2001.

In spite of the expansion of opportunities for girls' education in independent India, the situation of girl's education has not improved much. Illiteracy in our country is more pronounced among women than among men. Out of every four women, three are illiterate as compared to less than one out of every two men. The lower enrolment of girls in schools has been one of the major problems of our educational system, and a concerted

Issues and Problems in the Sociology of Jammu & Kashmir

effort is required to increase the enrolment of girls in schools so that we can achieve the desired goal of universalization of primary education. It thus requires a proper understanding of the disparities in girls' and boys' education, regional variations in girls' enrolment ratios and the possible factors associated with the low levels of girls' enrolment in schools.

Important Committees and Commissions on Girls' Education

The Secondary Education Commission (1952-1953) upheld opening of every type of education to women open to men.

Report of the Durgabai Deshmukh Committee on National Committee on Women's Education (1958-59) recommended:

- Appointment of school mothers in all schools where there is no woman teachers;
- Separate lavatory arrangement in every co-educational school;
- Help in cash or kind such as covering the cost of books and stationery; school uniform or clothing and other educational equipments to all girls upto middle level, whose parents are below certain level of income;
- Crèches for siblings;
- Schemes for awarding prizes to the villages which show the largest proportional enrolment and average attendance of girls;
- Attendance scholarships in the form of useful articles to poor girls
- Creation of strong public opinion for girls' education;
- Provisions of suitable conditions in schools rather than passing of compulsory legislation so that parents can be encouraged to send their daughters to schools;
- Women heads in coeducation schools.

Towards Equality: Report of the Committee on the Status of Women in India (1962-63) suggested incentives to prevent dropout among girls.

The Committee to look into the Causes of Lack of Public Support Particularly in Rural Areas, for Girls' Education and to Enlist Public Cooperation, 1963 and Committee on Differentiation of Curricula for Boys and Girls, 1964focussed on appointment of women teachers; appointment of women teachers; appointment of women teachers on staff should be obligatory where girls do attend middle school ordinarily meant for boys, and grant of free books, writing materials and clothing to girls.

The Education Commission (1964-66) fully endorsed the recommendations of National Committee on the Education of Women. The Commission emphasized on the following points;

- Appointing women teachers;

Issues and Problems in the Sociology of Jammu & Kashmir

- Popularizing mixed primary schools; and opening separate school for girls at the higher primary stage, wherever possible and demanded;
- Providing free books and writing material and if needed clothing also.

Towards an Enlightened and Humane Society NPE, 1986- A Review Committee for Review of National Policy on Education, 1986 in 1990upheld the need for adequate support services (water, fuel, fodder and child care) to the promotion of girls' education and more provisions of schooling facilities like atleast one primary school in each habitation with a population of 300 or more and atleast one middle school in each habitation with a population of 500 or more.

The National Perspective Plan for Women (1988-2000) recommended for women's education on the top priority basis so that women can attain a comparable level of education by 2000. The plan suggested that:

- Educational programmes need to be restructured and school curricula to be modified to eliminate gender bias.
- Awareness needs to be generated among the masses regarding the necessity of educating girls.
- Fifty percent posts in elementary schools should be reserved for women teachers. In every school, at least one woman teacher should be there.

REFERENCES

- ❖ Afzal, S.M and Shakeel Ahmad.2008.Students Enrolment in Higher Education: A Gender Comparison, *University News*, 46(30), July 28- August 03.

- ❖ Agarwal, Archana. 1992. A Study of some Educational problems of Scheduled Caste students. *The Indian Journal of Educational Research*, 19(1), 37-44.

- ❖ Agarwal, J.C. 1993. *Development and Planning of Modern Education*. New Delhi: Vikas Publishing House.

- ❖ Anand, Meena. 2005. *Dalit Women: Fear and Discrimination*. Delhi: Isha Books.

- ❖ Anand, Milind Roy. 2008. Visualising Girls in Unconvetional Roles: Myth or Reality, *Journal of Indian Education*, February: 89-96.

- ❖ Apple, Michael W. 1986. *Ideology and Curriculum*. London and New York: Routledge and Kegan Paul.

- ❖ Atal, Yogesh. 1979. *The Changing Frontiers of Caste*. New Delhi: National Publishing House.

- ❖ Bailey, F.G. 1957. *Caste and Economic Frontier*. Orissa: Manchester University Press.

- ❖ Barrett, M and A. Phillips. 1992. *Destabilizing Theory (ed.)*.Cambridge: Polity Press

- ❖ Bhadra, Mita. 1999. *Girl Child in Indian Society*. New Delhi: Rawat Publications.

- ❖ Bhattacharya, Sabyasachi. 2002. *Education and the Disprivileged: Nineteenth and Twentieth Century India (ed.)*. New Delhi: Orient Longman Private limited.

- ❖ Bhushan, Sudhanshu. 2006. *Higher Education: Resconstructing from the Past and Reconstituting the New*. Lecture delivered at Orientation Programme, 24 February 2006-24 March 2006, CPDHE, University of Delhi, Delhi.

- ❖ Bourdieu, Pierre and Jean-Claude Passeron.1977. *Reproduction in education, society and Culture*. London: Sage Publication.

- ❖ Chanana, Karuna. 2001. *Interrogating women's education : bounded visions, expanding horizons*. Jaipur: Rawat Publications.

- ❖ Chandana, R.C. 1992. *A Geography of Population*. New Delhi: Kalyani Publishers.

- ❖ Chauhan, B.R. 1967. Special Problems Regarding Education among the Scheduled Castes in M.S Gore (et.al.eds), *Papers in the Sociology of Education in India*, New Delhi.

- ❖ Chohan, Amar Singh. 1998. *Development of Education in Jammu and Kashmir State* (1846-1947). Jammu: Atlantic Publishers and Distributors.

❖ Dumont, Louis. 1988. *Homo Hierarchicus: The Caste System and its Implications*, Delhi: Oxford University Press, First Pub. 1966.

❖ Durkheim, Emile. 1956. *Education and Sociology*. New York: The Free Press.

❖ Ghosh and Ghosh. 1997. *Dalit Women*. New Delhi: A.P.H. Publishing Corporation.

❖ Ghurye, G.S. 1957. *Caste and Class in India*. Bombay: Popular Prakshan, First Pub. 1950.

❖ Glifford, James and Gabrielle Zezulka Mailloux. 2003. *Culture + the State: Alternative Interventions*. Canada: CRC Humanities.

❖ Goswami, B. 2003. *Constitutional Safeguards for Schedule Caste and Schedule Tribes*. Jaipur: Rawat Publications.

❖ Gupta, Dipankar. 1991. *Social Stratification: Continuous Hierarchies and Discrete Castes*. New Delhi: Oxford University Press.

❖ Guru, Gopal. 1995. Dalit Women Talk Differently, in *Economic and Political Weekly*, Vol: 30, No. 41/42.

❖ Jain, Devaki and Pam Rajput. 2003. *Narratives from the Women's Studies Family (ed)*. New Delhi: Sage Publications.

❖ Jeffrey, Craig and et al. 2005. 'When Schooling Fails: Young Men, education and Low Caste Politics in Rural North India' in *Contribution to Indian Sociology* (n.s.), Vol. 39, No.7, pp. 1-38.

❖ Jha, J.K. 2002. *Status of Girl Child in India*. New Delhi: Sarup and Sons.

❖ Jogdand, P. G. 1995. *Dalit Women in India: Issues and Perspectives*. New Delhi: Gyan Publishing House.

❖ Judge, S.Paramjit.1993.Scheduled Caste Women in Work Force in Rural Punjab, *in Ambedkar Journal of Social Development and Justice*, Vol:3.

❖ Kapadia, K.M. 1995. *Marriage and Family in India*. Bombay: Oxford University Press.

❖ Keer, D. 1964. *Mahatma Jyotirao Phule – The Father of Our Social Revolution*. Bombay: Popular Parkshan Pvt. Ldt.

❖ Kripal, Vinay. 1978. Higher Education for the Scheduled Castes and Scheduled Tribes, *Economic and Political Weekly, Vol.13 (4&5), pp. 165-169.*

❖ Kumar, Vijandra. 2000. *Rise of Dalit Power in India*. Jaipur: ABD Publishers.

❖ Kumar, Vivek. 2006. *India's Roaring Revolution: Dalit Assertion and New Horizons*. Delhi: Gagandeep Publications

❖ Mahey, Sonia. 2003. The State of Dalit Women in India's Caste Based System, in James. Glifford, and Gabrielle Zezulka Mailloux (eds.), *Culture + the State: Alternative Interventions* (pp.149-54). Canada: CRC Humanities.

❖ Malik, Bela. 1999. Untouchability and Dalit Women's Oppression, in *Economic and Political Weekly*, Vol:34, No. 6, February.

❖ Mandal. 1980. *Mother and Girl Child: Reconstructing Attitudes*. New Delhi: Rawat Publications.

❖ Mishra, R.C. 2005.*Women Education*. Kul Bhushan Nangia: APH Publishing Corporation.

❖ Muthumarry, J. 2000. *Dalit Women in India*. Paper presented at the international Dalit Human Rights Conference, London 16-17 September.

❖ Office of the Registrar General of India.(2001). Census of India, India.

❖ Pandey, Balaji .1986. Educational Development Among Scheduled Castes, in *Economic and Political Weekly*, Vol.14, No.2/3.

❖ Parsons, Talcott. 1968. The School Class as a Social System: Some of its Function in American Society' in Robert R. Bell and Holger R. Stub (eds.): *The Sociology of Education: A Source Book*, (pp. 199-218). Homewood: The Dorsey.

❖ Paswan, Sadanand.2001. *Dalitsand Practices of Untouchability*. New Delhi: Adhyayan Publishers and Distributors.

❖ Pathak, Avijit. 2004. *Social Implications of Schooling: Knowledge, Pedagogy and Consciousness*. Delhi: Rainbow Publishers.

❖ Rajawat, Mamta. 2003. *Scheduled Castes in India (ed.)*. New Delhi: Anmol Publications Pvt. Ltd.

❖ Rajawat, Mamta. 2005. *Dalit women Issues and Perspectives*. New Delhi: Anmol Publications. Pvt. Ltd

❖ Ram, Nandu. 1995. *Beyond Ambedkar: Essays on Dalits in India*. New Delhi: Har Anand Publications.

❖ Ramaswamy,Uma. 1974. Self Identity Among Scheduled Castes: A study of Andhra, *Economic and Political Weekly*, Vol.9, No.48.

❖ Ranadive, B.T. 1979. Caste, Class and Property Relation, *in Economic and Political Weekly*, Vol. 14, No. 7/8.

❖ Rao, Anupama. 2003. *Issues in Contemporary Indian Feminism: Gender and Caste (ed.)*. New Delhi: Kali for Women.

❖ Rao, Chinna Yagati. 2007. *Writing Dalit History and other Essays*. New Delhi: Kanishka Publishers.

❖ Reddy, P. Adinaryana.D.Uma Devi and E. M. Reddy.2009. *Education of the Scheduled Castes*. Ambala Cantt: The Associated Publishers.

❖ Reddy, P.R. and P. Sumangala.1998.*Women in Development: Perspectives from Selected States of India*, Vol. II .New Delhi: B.R Publishing Corporation.

❖ Reddy, R.C. 1986.*Changing Status of Educated Working Women towards Marriage and Family*.New Delhi: B.R Cooperation Publications.

Issues and Problems in the Sociology of Jammu & Kashmir

❖ Rege, Sharmila. 1998. Dalit women talk differently: A Critique of Difference and Towards a Dalit feminist standpoint Position, in *Economic and Political Weekly*, Vol.33, No. 44, October 31-November 6.

❖ Roy Burman, B.K., B. Choudhuri and K.K.Mishra (ed).2004. *Encylopedia of Indian Tribes and Castes* (Vols. 12:3594-97 & 16: 4726-38). New Delhi: Cosmo Publications.

❖ Sachchidananda .1974.Studies of Scheduled Castes with special reference to change, ICCSR, in *Survey of Research in Sociology and social Anthropology*, Vol: I. Bombay: Popular Prakashan.

❖ Saxena, Ashish. 2007. Another Leap towards Land Reforms in J&K, in *Mainstream*,Vol: X11, No. 40, September.

❖ Saxena, Ashish. 2009. *Shifting Manifestations : Scheduled Castes in Jammu and Kashmir. Jammu*:Saksham Books.

❖ Seru, S.L. 1973. *History and Growth of Education in Jammu and Kashmir*, 1872-1973. Srinagar: Ali Mohammad Publication.

❖ Shah, A.M.,Bhbaviskar, B.S.,Ramaswamy, E.A. 1996. *Social Structure and Change, Women in Indian Society*, Vol-2. New Delhi: Sage Publications

❖ Shah, Ghanshyam. 2006. *Untouchability in Rural India*. New Delhi: Sage Publications.

❖ Shah, Ganshayam.2002.Education and Backward Castes in Gujarat, in Sabyasachi Bhattacharya (ed.): *Education and the Disprivileged: Nineteenth and Twentieth Century India* (pp. 255-269). New Delhi: Orient Longman Private limited

❖ Sharma, Seema and Kanta Sharma. 2006. *Dalit and Backward Women*. New Delhi: Anmol Publications Pvt. Ltd.

❖ Singh, S.K.2000. *Dalit Women: Socio-economic Status and Issue*. New Delhi: New Royal Book Corporation.

❖ Smelsor, Neil J. 1993. *Sociology*. New Delhi (Fourth edition).

❖ Sorokin, P.A. 1927. *Social and Cultural Mobility* : Harper and Brothers

❖ Srivastava, Vinay Kumar (ed.). 2004. *Methodology and Fieldwork*. New Delhi: Oxford University Press.

❖ Swaminathan, M.S. 1982. Educational development of Scheduled Caste, *in Journal of Indian Education, 8(1), May, pp.40-55.*

❖ Swaminathan, P.2008. Exclusions from Inclusions in Development: Implications for Engendering Development, in *Economic and Political Weekly*, 25 October: 48-56.

❖ Thorat, Sukhadeo.2009. *Dalits in India: Search for a Common Destiny*. New Delhi: Sage Publications India Pvt. Ltd.

❖ Thorat, S.K.1996. *Dalit and the New Economic Policy*in *Dalit International Newsletter*, 1(2).

❖ Thorat, S.K. and Deshpande R.S. 1998.*Economic Theories of Caste System: A Review Paper Presented on Ambedkar, in Retrospect.* New Delhi: Jawaharlal Nehru University.

❖ Wankhede, G.G. 1999. *Social Mobility and Scheduled Caste.* Jaipur and New Delhi: Rawat Publications.

❖ Wankhede, G. G. 2001. Educational Inequalities Among Schedule Castes in Maharashtra, *Economic and Political Weekly*, Vol. 36, No. 18, pp. 1553-58, 05-11 May.

❖ Zelliot , Eleanor. 1996. *From Untouchable to Dalit:* Essays on the Ambedkar Movement: New Delhi.

Reports and Journals

❖ IMPA, 2008. A DFID-GOI Project Report on Education Sector in Jammu and Kashmir State, Institute of Management, Public Administration and Rural Development, Srinagar.

❖ Jammu and Kashmir, Government of. 2009. *Economic Survey 2008-09.* Jammu: Directorate of Economic and Statistics; Planning and development.

❖ Jammu and Kashmir, Government of. *Digest of Statistics 2000-07.* Jammu: Directorate of Economic and Statistics

❖ Ramakrishna, A.S. 1992. Education for Equality, *Journal of Social Welfare*, 39: 7-10.

❖ Sharp, Henry.1916. *A note on Education in the State of Jammu and Kashmir* ,Suptt, Government Printing Press, Calcutta, (Photo Copy available in State Archive Library, Jammu 1956) pp. 37-38; Hari Om, Muslim Jammu and Kashmir. New Delhi: Archives Publishers.

CHAPTER-IX

A SOCIOLOGICAL STUDY OF SOCIETY IN LADAKH

AN ANTHROPOLOGICAL OVERVIEW

TSERING JOLDEN

Introduction

The state of Jammu and Kashmir is divided into three divisions Jammu, Kashmir and Ladakh. Leh (77% Buddhist) and Kargil (80% Muslim) are two districts of Ladakh, bifurcated in 1979. Leh district comprises of Leh town and 113 villages. About 75.57% population of Leh district lives in villages. Leh is the largest district of Jammu and Kashmir state spreading over an area of 45,110 sq. km forming 44.49% land area of the state (Leh District Statistical Handbook)[1]. According to 2011 census, the population of Leh district was 1,47,104 persons. It is one of the least populated districts of the country having lowest density of population, nearly 3 persons per sq. km. Leh district also has the lowest sex ratio i.e. 583* in Jammu and Kashmir according to 2011 census. Decline in sex ratio started during the decade of 70's and continued in 80's. According to census of 1971, the sex ratio of Leh district was 1,002 and it declined to 886 in the year 1981 and it became 823 in 2001 census (Census of India, 2011)[2].

Some twenty-five hundred years ago, the rich culture of India also gave rise to Buddhism. Today more than 330 million people (6 percent of humanity) have embraced Buddhism, and almost all are Asian (Macionis, 1987)[3]. There are different opinions regarding introducing of Buddhism in Ladakh. According to Cunningham, Buddhism penetrated into Ladakh from Kashmir during the reign of emperor Ashoka in the 243 B.C. and so was the first Buddhist temple set up in Suru valley during his reign. The village of Sumda and Tiri still have attributed to Ashoka while the Kanika stupa at Sanni in Zanskar is said to have materialized through force of Ashoka's prayers. However, some have attributed construction of this stupa to the king Kaniska in the 2nd century A.D. who is believed to have annexed Ladakh and Baltistan to his vast empire. Luciano Petech holds the view that Buddhism penetrated into Ladakh from Kashmir during the Kushan's period and due to drass proximity to Kashmir the influence of Kashmir prevailed for a long time as testified by the imposing sculptures of Maitraya and Avalokiteskwara there (Kaul, 1998)[4].

The spread of Buddhism, as is universally known, owes much to the missionary zeal of Emperor Ashoka who spared no efforts in propagating the teaching of the Buddha in the neighbouring countries including Ladakh at the close of the third Buddhist council held in Patlipura to discuss measures for propagation of the Dharma. During Kaniska's rule starting from 78 A.D. the roots of Buddhism strengthened further in Ladakh. Kaniska called the fourth Buddhist Council at Kundalavana in Kashmir to discuss some important question about Buddhism. The council was attended by many famous scholars like Nagarjuna, Ashvagosha and Vasumitra. During Kaniska's rule, Buddhism split into two sects namely the Hinayana and Mahayana. Buddhism flourished in Ladakh ever since and with the establishment of the institution of the Dalia Lama as the supreme spiritual and temporal authority of Tibet, Ladakh came under the religious influence of Lhasa (ibid)[5]. Buddhism comes to Ladakh probably from both Tibet and Kashmir (Hodge, 1991)[6]. Buddhism is a minority religion in India as well as in Jammu and Kashmir.In Ladakh there are eight type of tribes which are *Balti, Beda, Bot, Brokpa, Changpa, Gara, Mon* and *Purigpa*. Of which *Brokpa, Balti* and *Purigpa* are found mostly in Kargil district. The people of Ladakh got the status of Schedule Tribe in the year 1989. Due to their isolation from others parts of country, they have been deprived of many benefits but with the advancement of time they have been drifting into mainstream. The Central and State governments have undertaken various steps to improve their conditions.

Numerically the tribes in India are a small segment of the total population but culturally they have made significant contribution to the identity of pan-Indian culture. The tribal people are characterized by their ethnic sensitivities and distinct socio-economic practices (Saxena, 2008)[7].

All the social, cultural and religious organizations were very active politically and with their political and collective struggles were successful in achieving the ST (Scheduled Tribe) status for whole of the Ladakh region and in October 1989, the State Government of Jammu And Kashmir passed a state order number SRO-GSR 882, by order of His Excellency, the President of India Shri R. Venkataraman declared the Scheduled tribe status for the whole of Ladakh (Sharma, 2001)[8].

History and Origin of the People

The Buddhist element of the population comprises different ethnic groups, the earliest settlers being the Dards who emigrated from Dardistan in Gilgit region century back. The mons belong to the Aryans stock came next from Kullu side and the last wave of immigrants rolled into the land from Tibet side and provided the predominant Mongolian strand to the racial mosaic of the land. The aristocratic families of Skardu in occupied Kashmir claim descent from the Greek soldier Alexander the Great whose army they claim marched through their land into the Indian plains. Ladakh, as we know, was the nerve-centre of the Central Asian trade when many a family from Chinese, Turkistan settled their thus adding another racial element to the population. Similarly, in pursuit of commercial interests, some Kashmiri popularly known as 'Argon' also settled in Ladakh, mainly in the towns, whose blood eventually mixed up with that of the earlier settlers. The demographic profile of Ladakh which emerge from intermingling of all these heterogeneous elements can thus be classified under some broad divisions, the Bot, the Changpas, the Mons, the Bedas, and the Garas (Kaul, 1998)[10].

The blending process started when Ladakh was the transit point on the Central Asian trade route where the traders, nomads and invaders from Yarkand, Baltistan, Punjab, Kashmir, China, Tibet, etc. used to pass through Ladakh. Some settled here permanently while some had temporary homes and got married with the local girls which gave the present stock of population of Ladakh. The inter-mixing of local women with Muslims and Hindus is the current trend in changing the Ladakhi breed. The people of Muslim dominated Kargil have sharp features akin to the Kashmiris which is the result of marriage between local women and merchants from Kashmir (Bhasin, 2006)[11].

Buddhism penetrated Ladakh during Emperor Asoka's time in 204 B.C. However, the Buddhist practice in Ladakh was not the same then as it is today. The form of Buddhism which is popularly called Mahayana Buddhism came to Ladakh with the blessing of the land by the great Buddhist saint Padmasambhava in the eighth century A.D. It was Padmasambhava who, along with the great Bhikhu Santaraksita, firmly established Buddhism during the reign of the most powerful Tibetan emperor Trison Detsen. Ever since that time, the people of Tibet have followed the religion of the Buddha. The Tibetans and others who follow what we now call Tibetan Buddhism including many Ladakhis regard three great pioneers with a sense of deep gratitude and admiration (Shakspo, 2010)[12].

Geographically, the area Ladakh may be divided into seven parts: Sham (lower), Tod (upper), Zhung (centre), Nubra, Changthang, Purig, and Zanskar. All these seven parts of Ladakh have distinctive cultural and literary identities. For example, Zanskar, the southern part of Ladakh, has been called 'Chosyul', the 'Country of religion', because it has the highest literacy rate of all Ladakh, owing to its monastic traditions. Similarly, the northern part is called Nubra (Ldumra), the 'Garden of Flowers'. Buddhism is practice by the people there and Nubra boasts some of the finest monasteries of Ladakh. Various types of flowers blossom there and a celebration called the 'Festival of Flowers' (metog ldad mo) is held in spring. On this occasion, people perform various type of dance, presenting flowers in their hands as a gesture in the form of an offering to the Buddha.

As with Zanskar and Nubra there are certain peculiarities in the culture of every region of Ladakh. For instance the people of Changthang wear a distinctive dress which really suits the harsh climate (and high altitude) of the area (Shakspo, 2010)[13].

The language of Ladakh is called Bothi which is a modified version of the original Tibetan language with a mixture of Ladakhi and Tibetan vocabulary spoken with Ladakhi accent. The educated Ladakhi can read and write in Bothi or Tibetan but they speak Ladakhi dialect. The official language of Ladakh as well as of the state is Urdu. An educated Ladakhi can speak in Bothi, Urdu, Hindi and English. In the school curriculum, four languages are taught in Ladakh, i.e. Bothi, Hindi, Urdu and English. There are various dialects spoken in Ladakh like Balti, Kashmiri, Dardi, Shina, Shamme, Zanskari, Nubre, and Changpe (Bhasin, 2006)[14].

The interesting thing is that the Ladakhi are quite adept to understand each other's dialects which sometime carry very difficult pronunciation. The language spoken at and around Leh is considered as the standard Ladakhi language which is aired on radio and television in Leh. Balti is spoken in the villages of Chushot and Kargil. Shina is spoken in Drass valley and Dardi is spoken in Da and Hanu. Shamme is spoken by the lower altitude Sham areas. Being close to Tibet, the dialect of Changpas is relatively difficult as they derive the linguistic traits from Tibetan migrants. Tibetan is the toughest dialect, but, Ladakhi and Tibetans can understand most of their language, as there is a considerable population of Tibetan in Ladakh and their daily social interaction helps them to know each other's dialects (Shakspo, 2010)[15].

Social classes

The Ladakh Buddhist society is divided into three principal classes which are upper, middle and lower. The upper class is locally known as 'Rigzang' comprising Gyalpo (king), Kushok (head lama), Kalon (ministers) and Lonpo (governors). 'Mangrik' or the middle class includes Lamas and chomos (monks and nuns), Onpos (astrologers), Larje (physician) and common man. The lower class or 'Rignun' includes Beda (musicians), Mon (musicians), and Gara (blacksmiths). The Beda, Mon and Gara are considered as lower tribes like untouchables and no family relation like marriage are established among them by the upper and middle class. They have to find the matrimonial alliance in their own community. These three tribes can take food of a middle and upper class but upper and middle class could not take food from them. Earlier these rules are followed very strictly but now the people are little liberal in behaving with them.

During marriage and other functions there is arrangement of hierarchical sitting are made but the Mon, Beda and gara have to sit in the last whether they are senior or not by age. The choktse (Ladakhi table) is not provided to these people as a mark of distinction. The *bedas* and the *Mons* are musicians by profession who are given a piece of land by the villagers and in return they play music in every function held in the village.

Metal objects have always been a universal necessity and the blacksmiths, *gara*, form a distinct community, of which a few members are found in every village of Ladakh. The utilitarian objects of everyday use, like *thap* (chullah,) ploughshares, other agriculture implements and cooking pots, more decorative items like tea and chang pots, prayer wheel and others objects are made by *gara* tribes.

Elaborately the population of Leh district is categorized into the following distinct group:

1. Bot (majority in number)
2. Changpa (pastoralists of Highland)
3. Gara (blacksmiths)
4. Beda (musicians)
5. Mon (musicians)
6. Dogpa or brokpa (Aryan race)
7. Tibetans (Lately colonized in Leh)
8. Muslim (both Shia and Sunni)
9. Christian
10. Hindu
11. Sikh

Some of these groups follow specific occupation for instance Beda and Mon are musicians, the rest have more than one occupation. Religion wise population of Leh district as per 2001 census are Buddhist 77.30, followed by Muslim 13.78%, Hindus 8.16, Sikhs 0.43% and Christians 0.33%. Among all the religion 82.04% of population is Scheduled Tribe (Leh-District Statistical Handbook 2009-10)[16].

Polo and archery are the most popular and ancient sports of Ladakh. Polo is said to have been introduced into Ladakh from Baltistan where it was quite popular and the Balti princess Gyal Khatoon is said to have brought it into Ladakh when she became the Ladakhi queen. She is also stated to have brought the musical instruments like *'Daman'*(like tabla) and *'Surna'* (shennai), along with musicians, as a part of dowry. The polo grounds in Ladakh are located at Leh, Chushot, Drass and Kargil (Bhasin, 2006)[17].

Being a sandy and rocky land at high elevation, the soil is not much fertile and requires lots of water for irrigation, and sourcing the water either from river or from glacier is quite difficult and requires hard-work. The villages which are close to the river and the glacier-fed water channel are quite better off than the others. The climate is also not conductive for high yielding crops and consequently the fields are also not large. Most of the

Ladakhis possess at least a small piece of land on which farming is done and its produce is stored for their personal consumption around the year.

The soil condition of Leh and *Nubra* valley is favourable for high yielding crops as compared to *Changthang* area where the soil and extreme climate conditions are against the high yielding agriculture produce. A variety of crops is sown in Leh and around villages which is situated on the bank of the Indus River. The staple food of Ladakh is wheat and barley. A number of varieties in vegetables are also grown in Leh District. Among fruits, apple, apricot, grapes, walnuts, etc are grown at lower elevation.

Family and Marriage

Family and marriage are both universal social institutions and are closely associated with each other. Like other institutions, these institutions are also governed by certain values, rules, regulations, laws, customs and traditions. But these rules differ in different societies according to their customs and traditions. Due to their isolation from other parts of country, people of Leh also have different kind of marriage and family.

The present research has made an attempt to study marriage and family among Buddhists of Leh. There are many forms of mating relationships. Many scholars have written about family and marriage. There is mention of different forms of marriage like by Maclver and Page (1950)[18]. The mating relation may be lifelong or of shorter duration. It may take the institutional form of monogamy, which may be strict or modified by subsidiary sex relationships. It may be polygamous, involving either polygyny, the most highly regarded arrangement in many communities, or polyandry, an infrequent and unpopular variety. Even what seems a form of group marriage has been found in one or two primitive societies. A society may, in fact recognize more than one of these varieties, as among the Tibetans, where the economically depressed practiced polyandry, the better off, monogamy, and some of the wealthy nobles, polygyny.

Malinowski argues that marriage is a "contract for the production and maintenance of children". Families may be classified on the basis of norms pertaining to place of residence and relation of authority. A newly married couple may set up house together (Neolocal residence) as it is common norms practiced in the west today, the wife may move to live with her husband or with his parental kin (Virilocal or patrilocal residence respectively) or a man may move to live with his wife (Uxorilocal or matrilocal residence) (Palriwala and Uberoi, 2008)[19].

Family

All of us know about marriage and families. Parents, siblings, spouses, children these are not remote and academic subjects but virtually everyone's first hand experiences. Family is a social unit of which almost every one of us is a member. It is the most remarkable and one of the oldest of all our social institutions. Family organisation, however, is not instinctive. Nevertheless, it is found everywhere. The fact of universality can be taken for its functionality or usefulness to the personal and social needs. It influences the whole life of a society in innumerable ways, and any change in it reverberates through the entire social structure. It is capable of endless variations, and yet reveals a remarkable continuity and persistence. Society depends on the institution of family for the reproduction, protection, socialization and social placement of its members-function through its continuation as well as maintenance of social order is possible. In addition to these universal functions, the family performs important economic, social, educational, recreational and religious functions. For all these reasons family is called 'cradle of human nature' (Chakraborty, 2002)[20].

As a social unit, a family is defined as a group of persons of both sexes, related by marriage, blood or adoption, performing roles based on age, sex and relationship, and socially distinguished as making up a single household or a sub-house hold (Ahuja, 2006)[21]. The family is a group defined by a sex relationship sufficiently precise and enduring to provide for the procreation and upbringing of children. Family is the first and most influential setting for socialization (MacIver and Page, 1950)[22].

In Ladakh, families are known as 'Nang-tsangs'. Families in Ladakh are of two type *khangchen* (ancestor's house) and *khaou* (one who separated from ancestor's house). Separated families may be brothers, sisters (married or unmarried) as well as parents. The reason of separation might be to avoid mutual conflicts as well as due to mutual conflicts among the family members. When they stay away from each other chances of conflicts and quarrels are minimized.

Traditionally, there are more joint families and these days nuclear families are becoming more popular. Polyandry is gradually declining in Leh. Joint family also known as consanguine family is predominated in rural areas where as Nuclear family also known as conjugal family is more in towns because of migration. Descent is traced through bilateral descent, both patrilineal and matrilineal. In Ladakh one is identified by one's house name, there is no surname on the basis of caste. House name would be given according to the location, animal names, occupation during king's rule.

After marriage residence is either patrilocal, matrilocal or neolocal. From marriage perspective, the family can be classified into three categories namely monogamous, polygynous and polyandrous. There is preponderance of monogamous families, followed, in order, by polyandrous and rarely polygynous. Some of the characteristics of joint family do mark even the polyandrous families. For instance, the members of a polyandrous family have a common residence and jointly contribute to house economy.

An interesting and perhaps unique feature of the village life in Ladakh is the phaspun, an institution that even now gives solidarity and support to every Buddhist family. This is the grouping of between five to fifteen families bound together by their worship of common Lha, or deity. In Leh district, phaspun usually consists of related as well as unrelated families. The phaspun becomes operational on the major occasions of family life: birth, marriage and death, which involve large-scale entertaining of fellow villagers (Rizvi, 1996)[23].

This kind of system came into being during earlier times, when there was scarcity of money, food, liquor, etc. So that there will be cooperation between families during the time of birth, marriage and death. One of the superstitious beliefs of local people is that only phaspun members can eat or drink during birth and death. Phaspun work become more important during death ceremony because they have the responsibility of cooking for all the members as well as for monk who came there for performing religious rituals and the body of the decease are taken care by these members. The phaspun members also take care of the infants and animals of the deceased person.

Several sociologists' studies conducted in different parts of the country between 1950's and 1980's also indicate that the old-style joint family is rare and the nature of jointness is changing from that of 'residence' to one of 'fulfilling obligation'(Ahuja, 2006)[24]. The present study has also looked into the changes that are undergoing in the structure of family.

The traditional form of the joint family is changing its structure and function under the forces like urbanization and industrialization. People have migrated from villages to town. One way to characterize this change is to associate conjugal or nuclear forms of families with relatively modernized or industrial society and extended or joint types of families with traditional-agarian and pre-industrial societies (Singh, 1996)[25].

Some of the change is also being seen in the villages of Leh district. There are more mutual conflicts within the family especially between the mother-in-law and the daughter-in-law. These kinds of conflict are the reason for the change from joint to nuclear families. In the villages people are migrating from village to town for jobs and education. Education has also brought some changes. Students are migrating from village to town for their higher education. There are more possibilities of jobs in the town than in the villages so there are more neolocal types of residence in the town. There is also change in the type of occupation from agriculture to non-agriculture.

In Leh district there is a wide range of variation in the nature and pattern of family. All the inmates of a house sharing economic responsibilities and related through Kinship have been considered as a family. It may be mentioned that apart from family the individual members are also, at times, referred as "Nang-Changs" a term which correspond to the family. There exist family composed of only husband and wife. Then there are nuclear and extended families. The later exist in various forms.

R.S Mann (2002)[6] in his study of four villages of Leh district has shown the nature and pattern of Ladakhi family which can be represented in following categories.

1. Nuclear
2. Extended (three generational or more; it also include polyandrous families).
3. Joint.
4. Extended joint
5. Husband and wife (without children)
6. A widow staying alone
7. A deserted or divorced person living alone
8. A widower living alone
9. A wife and her two husbands
10. Husband, wife, daughter and her resident husband
11. Husband, wife, daughter and her resident husband and their children
12. Father, two daughters and their two resident husbands and children
13. Husband, wife and adopted son
14. Husband, wife and adopted daughter
15. Husband, wife adopted son and his wife and children
16. Husband, wife adopted daughter and her husband and children
17. Husband, wife children, including the deserted or divorced daughter
18. Husband, wife and her unmarried sister staying together.

From the above pattern of families, it is clear that the members belonging to different *Gyuts* (a term corresponding to Lineage) do stay together and make the constituent units of this social group. In normal course, the forms of Nang-Chang keep within the well defined and commonly accepted categories such as nuclear, joint, extended and extended joint. Mann in his study of four villages has shown the types of families- predominantly (49.0%) the families are of extended kind followed, in order, by the nuclear ones (31.67%). nearly 14.00% of the families belong to the category 'others' which are to be explained in their respective forms. The joint and extended joint families constituted 1.0% and 4.33% respectively. Average number of persons per family is 6.02.

Table2.1. Head of the Family

Family	No. of Respondents	Percentage (%)
1. Male Headed	51	85
2. Female Headed	09	15
Total	60	100

Out of 60 respondents 85% (48 respondents) are male headed and 15% (9 respondents) are women headed families. The families in which important decisions are taken by particular members and property is in his/her name are taken as head of the family. Most of the women headed families are in the case of 'Makpa' marriages.

Table no.2.2 Family type (Joint and Nuclear)

Type	No. of Respondents	Percentage (%)
Joint (3 or more generation)	23	38.33
Nuclear (1 or 2 generation)	37	61.67
Total	60	100

With the change from joint to nuclear family there is also decline in the age of head of the family. Out of 60 respondents 23 (38.33%) are living in a joint family and 37 (61.67%) respondents live in a nuclear family.

Traditional Buddhist House of Leh.

Marriage

With the abolishment of polyandry in 1941, like other societies, monogamous marriage has become popular in Leh district. Monogamous marriages in Ladakh are of two type *pagma* and *makpa*. It was found in the present research that there is presence of neolocal, virilocal and uxorilocal residences in the area under study. Neolocal types of residence are increasing in number in Leh district. While we can see many virilocal, which is the residence type followed in Pagma marriages, there are also uxorilocal residence which is the residence type followed in Magpa marriages in Leh.

1. Pagma marriage (Virilocal-where bride goes to groom's house).

2. Makpa marriage (Uxorilocal-Where groom goes to bride's house).

Makpa with Makrok (Groom maid)
Pagma with *Pakrok* (Bride maid)

Sports of Ladakh

The traditional sport of Ladakh is the archery competition. The people of Ladakh are fond of archery and often organize competition in almost every village during summer. The systematic organization of *'Dartses'* (archery competition) is itself an interesting feature. It includes amusement, entertainment, competition, community feeling and unity.

A day is fixed by 'Khak-Khur' (the responsible family) which is three or four families. Khak-khur is the organizer which comes to every family turn by turn. Some contributions in cash are raised from all the households of the village which is collected by the organizers. It is believed that archery is traditional custom which should be organized every year for the welfare of the village. The collected money is used for food, tea and chang. The competition accompanied by loud music, provided by the Mon and Beda. The musicians also earn money as they fixed money with every dance.

The place which is usually an open space in or around the village, and the day of the competition are then announced. The villagers turn up in high spirits with bow and arrow. On this occasion the men and women are nicely dressed in the traditional dress 'goncha'. Women sport their Perak and other ornaments on the occasion. A target to hit by the arrow is then fixed in a sand heap. A line on the ground is then marked at a distance of 15-20 yards from the target. All the bows and arrows are kept near this line.

The competition is between the individuals, as also between the teams. Fixed numbers of chances are given to each individual to hit the target. An experienced man is appointed as referee. The game of archery starts around in the morning with dance by both men and women and continues till the sun-set. With every hit, the person who hits the target is given 'khataks' and he has to perform traditional Ladakhi dance followed by other men and women. The cooking and serving of food and drinks is the responsibility of khak-khur families. The male participants keep on sipping chang and females drink butter tea and milk tea as and when required. Towards the close of the competition the men and the women dance with the loud singing. Such a group dance marks the end of function.

The archery competitions are also organized by the religious persons. The kushok (head of monastery) and lamas (monks) organize archery competition for two days. The kushok inaugurates it by shooting first arrow at the target. A Mon and Beda are asked to come for performing their traditional music. Some villagers help the lamas in the preparation of tea and food. The religious men would sit in line keeping in view their seniority.

BIRTH AND DEATH RITUALS
Birth Ceremony
The birth of a child is a special occasion in the life of parents, so are the rituals attached with it. Earlier in villages of Ladakh no medical facilities were available; therefore, giving birth was always a risky affair. People believed that prayers would help to make the births safe and easy. Accordingly they request a village monastery's monk to frequently perform rituals for safe child birth. With the availability of medical facilities in far flung places, this ritual is declining these days. In Ladakh, the custom of rejoicing birth is somewhat elaborate and unique. The birth of a child,

Issues and Problems in the Sociology of Jammu & Kashmir

whether it is male or female, is a time of rejoicing with great fanfare. The newborn is given a name by the head monk of the monastery as well as by deity.

As soon as the baby is born, an arrow, known as *Dhan-dar*, (lucky arrow) is fixed in the heap of grain which is kept in a pot, and this pot is placed near the head of the child on *choktse* (small table) for 30 days. The visitors, who want to see and bless the child, come with *'khataks'* (white or golden scarf which is auspicious Tibetan tradition for welcoming and also for the start of a good relationship) and place it over this arrow. The close relatives also bring new clothes for the baby. The seventh day of the birth is called *'Dun'*. During this period, the nearest relatives and friends visit the house to bless the baby. The first 30 days are treated as pollution period and nobody takes food in the house of the newborn except the family and the phaspun members.

Death Ceremony

The funeral of a layman generally terminates, where circumstances allow of it, in the burning of the body, although the practice of exposing the corpse on the hill as a prey to the wild animals, formerly a very common one, is even now sometimes resorted to on account of the scarcity of wood. The ceremony of burning the body is performed upon an altar of a cubical form, in larger towns several of these are kept ready for immediate use, thus there are twelve such altars at Leh, surrounding the burial ground. In the countries where wood is plentiful, as in Bhutan and Sikkim, enough is employed to render the combustion complete, nothing remaining but ashes, but in Tibet it often happens that quantities of the bones remain unconsumed, which are then carefully collected, together with the ashes, and buried (Schlagintweit, 2008)[11].

The Phaspun has an important role during death ceremonies also. On occurrence of a death, one of the members of phaspun calls the monks from the monastery. They also give the news to other relatives. At the deceased person's house, a large party of monks assembles and the prayers are recited daily until the body is burned, which can take 4-8 days. The fourth day of deceased is important, because it is believe that the body is completely die on that day. All the rituals are performed by monks. During the course of prayer monks are given daily food and tea. While the dead body remains in the house, a piece of cloth is fixed over the door symbolizing the mourning. All the relatives and friends then visit the people in whose house death has occurred to show their sympathy by asking their relatives not to weep for their loss and they offer *taggi* (roti) or biscuits to console them

REFERENCES

Amiteshwar Ratra, Parveen Kaur and Sudha Chhikara. (2006): *Marriage and Family: In Diverse and Changing Scenario*. New Delhi: Deep and Deep Publications.

A. M Shah. (1998): *The Family in India: A Critical Essay*. New Delhi: Published by Orient Longman Limited.

Bron B. Ingoldsby, Suzanne R. Smith and J. Elizabeth Miller (2004): *Exploring Family Theories*. Los Angeles: Roxbury Publishing Company.

C. G Hussain Khan. (1994): *Marriage and Kinship among Muslim in South India*. Jaipur: Rawat Publication.

Emile Durkheim. (1984): *Division of Labour*. London: Mac Million Publications.

Francis Abraham. M. (2006): *Contemporary Sociology: An Introduction to Concept and Theories*. New Delhi: Oxford University Press.

Grace Don Namching. (2008): *Marriage, Family and Kinship among the Paite Tribe of Manipur*. New Delhi: Concept Publishing Company.

Gurnam Saran Bhatnagar. (1972): *Education and Social Change*. Calcutta: The Minerva Associates.

I.P. Desai. (1955): 'An Analysis Symposium on Caste and Joint family'. *Sociological Bulletin*, IV (2): pp. 97-117.

John Scott and Gordon Marshall (2005): *Oxford Dictionary of Sociology*. New York: Oxfrod University Press.

John J. Macionis (1997): *Sociology Sixth Edition*. New Jersey: Kenyon College Prentice-Hall International, Inc.

Madan and Majumdar (1985): *An Introduction to Social Anthropology*. Noida: Saraswati Printing Press.

M.N Srinivas. (1951): *Religion and Society among the Coorgs of South India*. Bombay: Asia Publishing House.

Nawang Tsering Shakspo. (2010): *A Cultural History of Ladakh*. Leh-Ladakh: The Solitarian, Centre for Research on Ladakh.

Pauline Kolenda (2003): *Caste, Marriage and Inequality: Essay on North and South India*. Jaipur: Rawat Publication.

R.S. Mann. (2002): *Ladakh Then and Now: Culture, Ecological and Political*. New Delhi: Mittal Publications.

S.C. Dube. (1955): *Indian Village*. London: Routledge and Kegan Paul Publications.

Schlaginweit, Emil. (2008). *Buddhism in Tibet*. Delhi: Sri Satguru Publications.

Smiriti Srinivas. (1994): 'Kindered and Political Patriliny: Two Style in Extra-Local Integration in Nubra Valley Ladakh'. *Sociological Bulletin*, Volume 43, Number 2, September, pp. 193-213.

Tulsi Patel (2005): *Family in India: Structure and Practice*. New Delhi: Sage Publications.

End Notes:

1. Yogender Singh. (1996) *Modernization of Indian Tradition*. Jaipur: Rawat Publication.

2. S.L Doshi. (2003) *Modernity, Post-modernity and Neo-Sociological Theories*. Jaipur: Rawat Publications.

3. Ibid.

4. David.L Snellgrove and Tadeusz Skorupski. (1977): *The Cultural Heritage of Ladakh*. New Delhi: Vikas publishing House.

5. Parvez Devan. (2004) *Jammu Kashmir and Ladakh*. New Delhi: Manas Publication.

6. Vidya Sagar Sharma. (2001) *Ladakh and Himalayas: Tourist and Spiritual Profile*. New Delhi: Anmol Publication.

7. H.N. Kaul. (1998) *Rediscovery of Ladakh*. New Delhi: Indus Publishing Company.

8. Nawang Tsering Shakspo. (2010) *A Cultural History of Ladakh*. Leh-Ladakh: Centre for Research on Ladakh: The solitarian.

9. Singh op.cit.ref.1.

10. Awadhesh Kumar Lal. (1990): *Urban Family*, New Delhi: Concept Publication Company.

11. John Scott and Gordon Marshall. (2004). *Oxford Dictionary of Sociology*. New York: Oxford University Press.

12. Dewan op.cit.ref.5.

13. International Association for Ladakh Studies (2009): *Ladakh Studies*, NR. 24June 2009.

14. Helena Norberg Hodge (1991): *Ancient futures learning from Ladakh*, New Delhi: Oxford University Press.

15. Maj. M.L.A. Gompertz. (1928) *Magic Ladakh: An Intimate Picture of a Land of Topsy-Turvy Custom and Great Natural Beauty*. Kashmir: Gulshan Books (reprinted in 2009).

16. Sanjeev Kumar Bhasin. (2006) *Amazing Land Ladakh: Places, People and Culture*. New Delhi: Indus Publishing Company.

17. Amiteshwar Ratra, Praveen Kaur, and Sudha Chhikara. (2006) *Marriage and family in diverse changing Scenario*, New Delhi: Deep and Deep Publications.

18. Kaul op.cit.ref.7.

Journals Cited

- Desai, I.P. 1955. An Analysis Symposiums on Caste and Joint family. *Sociological Bulletin*, IV (2).

- International Association for Ladakh Studies. *Ladakh Studies NR. 24 June 2009*. pp. 16.

- Saxena, Ashish.   2008. 'Tradition and Change among the Tribal Gujjar and Jammu Siwaliks' *Eastern Anthropology*, volume 61, Oct-Dec, New Delhi: Serial Publications.

- Smriti, Srinivas. 1994. 'Kindred and Political Patriliny: Two Style in Extra-local Integration in Nubra Valley, Ladakh,' *Sociological Bulletin*, volume 43, September-pp. 193-213.

Other Sources: Official/Un-official

Issues and Problems in the Sociology of Jammu & Kashmir

- Government of Jammu and Kashmir: Ladakh Autonomous Hill Development Council, Leh. *Statistical Hand Book for the year 2009-10.*

- Government of Jammu and Kashmir: Ladakh Autonomous Hill Development Council, *Leh District at A Glance series 14 (District Leh in J&K economy) 2008-09.*

- Census of India 2011, *Jammu and Kashmir* provisional population total 2011, Farooq Ahmed, I.A.S Director of Census operations, Jammu and Kashmir.

- Census of India 1981, *Jammu and Kashmir General Population Table- Series 8.* Jammu and Kashmir.

Websites
- http://en.wikipedia.org/wikijammuandkaslunir

- http;//Lehgov.nic.in

CHAPTER-X

INVESTIGATING CULTURE AND TRADITION IN ARCHITECTURE

A SOCIO HISTORICAL STUDY OF HINDU TEMPLES OF KASHMIR VALLEY IN J & K INDIA

DR. MUDASIR A. LONE
&
RAMEEZ AHMAD MIR

INTRODUCTION

Geologists believe that about ten crore years have passed when Kashmir Valley which was once a lake called Satisar, the lake of goddess Sati, came into its present form. For hundreds of millions years Kashmir Valley remained under Tethya sea and the high sedimentary-rock hills seen in the valley now were once under water. Geologists have come to believe that Kashmir Valley was earlier affected by earthquakes[1]. Once there was such a devastating earthquake that it broke open the mountain wall at Baramulla. and the water of the Satisar lake flowed out leaving behind lacustrine mud on the margins of the mountains known as Karewas. Thus came into existance the oval but irregular Valley of Kashmir. The Karewas being in fact the remanants of this lake confirm this view. The Karewas are found mostly to the west of the river Jhelum where these table-lands attain a height of about 380 meters above the level of the Valley. These Karewas protrude towards the east and look like tongue-shaped spurs with deep ravines.

Ancient legends and popular traditions say that Samdimat Nagar, capital of the kingdom of Sundra Sena, was submerged as a result of an earthquake and the water that filled the area formed the Wular Lake, the largest fresh water lake in India. The oldest igneous rocks are still found at Shankaracharya hill. When the whole Valley of Kashmir was under water this hillock was the first piece of dry land lying in the form of an igneous island. The temple builders of Kashmir were way ahead of their contemporaries of the plains and peninsular India. The 8th century Temples of Kashmir were constructed of evenly dressed ashlars masonry. Built of mammoth boulders, the joints were put together with lime mortar, which is seen at Wangat and also using steel dowels, used in the Martand

---

2. Sodhi S Lakhinder Singh, The History of Ancient Kashmir. p.p, 10

temple. These engineering developments were in vague in the neighboring Western region of Kashmir.

Si-Yu-Ki

Among the various travelogues, Huin-Tsangs[2]. Si-YU-Ki or records of the western world is regarded to be the most valuable source book for the study of ancient Indian history.Si-Yu-Ki is not merely a travel diary regarding Hiun-Tsang visited to various places in India during the seventh century, this journey was undertaking by Huin-Tsang primarily with a view to visiting the Buddhist places of pilgrimage and to seek answer to the question agitating his mind. He was inspired in this way by the recollection of similar journeys undertaken centuries ago by his predecessors, Fa-Hien, Sung-Yun and many others.

Born at Layiang in the year 600A.D. Huin-Tsang set out on his journey to regions west of China at the age of twenty nine in 629A.D. from Chang in west China.Huin-Tsang reached Kashmir during the reign of king *Durlabhavardhana* (627-649).Huin-Tsangs long account of Kashmir provides us interesting information about the contemporary religious conditions of Kashmir, there are both heretics and believers among them. However Hiuen-Tsangs account of Kashmir becomes more significant in view of its import for reconstructing the Kashmir history.

Kashmiri Authors

This splendid array of authoritative guides begins with the Nilamatapurana and continues practically without break to the present time. The age of the Nilamata is uncertain; but there is evidence to show that in one form or the other it was extant in the early Middle Ages. Beginning with the legend regarding the lacustrine origin of the valley and its drainage after the death of Jalodbhava, the water demon, who infested the lake and made human habitation on its shores impossible, the Purana gives us a detailed list of the holy places of Kashmir. To each name it appends a more or less comprehensive topographical description, which is of great value in identification of the numerous places mentioned.

By far the greatest amount of our information regarding ancient and mediaeval Kashmir is supplied by indigenous historians, of whom Kalhana is the oldest and most informative. He composed his Rajatarangini, the river of kings, in A.D. 1148-49[3]. Born in a Brahman official family, and learned in the traditions of his country both from oral and written sources, Kalhana was specially fitted for his self-imposed task, which he has executed with conspicuous ability. His father, Champaka, was the minister of king Harsha (A.D. 1089-1101), but after the murder of his master in

---

3. Beal, Life of Hieun Tsang, p.p. 69

4.Stein M.A, Rajtranigini, Trans. Vol.ii, p.p351-385

A.D. 1101 neither father nor son appears to have taken office under the succeeding rulers. He had a keen, observant eye, considerable sense of humour, vivid poetic imagination, and extensive knowledge of human nature. His impartiality in according praise or blame to his royal contemporaries, no less than to the kings of the past, shows that he was no sycophant. Though by birth he was a worshipper of Siva, he respected other sects and religions almost as much as he did his own form of faith. It is from the seventh century A.D. that history in the modern sense begins this does not mean that the earlier part of the chronicle is on that account without interest. On the contrary, it has very great value, not only because it mentions the great historic names of Asoka, Kanishka, etc., but also because it presents us with a fairly detailed account of the general condition of the kingdom before we reach the centuries which immediately precede the time of Kalhana, and for which he had genuine oral and written information. The latter consisted of a number of ancient histories written before Kalhana's time, of which he appears to have made extensive use. Unfortunately all of them are now lost, especially when we bear in mind that Kalhana regarded himself primarily as a poet, and composed the Rajatarangini as a didactic poem for the edification of his countrymen. Kalhana's chronicle has been published, with an excellent translation, exhaustive introduction, numerous explanatory notes, and a valuable monograph on the ancient geography and coinage, etc., of Kashmir, by Sir Aurel Stein. This monumental work is indispensable for the proper understanding of the social and political conditions of pre-Muslim Kashmir.

Bilhana, the poet, who has been alluded to above, has also left in his Vikramankadevacharita a glowing picture of the beauties of Kashmir in general, besides giving a description of his rural home at Khunamusha, which is known today as the rakh (game preserve) of Khunamoh. The book known as the Lokaprakasa is a curious mixture of the ordinary dictionary and a practical handbook dealing with various topics of administration and private life in Kashmir. There are many monuments and heritage buildings of Kashmir till from earliest time's upto 1200 A.D.

Early temples in Kashmir

No structural monuments which can, with certainty, be said to belong to the pre-Christian era have yet been discovered in Kashmir. Even the first six centuries A.D. are very meagerly represented; the only monuments which can with certainty be assigned to the Kushan period being the Buddhist structures at Harwan and Ushkar[4].

---

5. Stein MA, Rajtarngini, trans, vol.i, p.p, 330

The abundance in which the coins of Indo-Greek, Parthian, and Saka kings of north-western India were found until recently in Kashmir points to the existence of considerable commercial intercourse, if not actual political connection, between the valley and the principalities of Peshawar and Kabul in the last two centuries B.C. and the first century A.D. It is also certain that in the second century A.D. Kashmir formed part of Kanishka's empire and that, for at least some generations after the death of that emperor, the country remained attached to the kingdom of Gandhara. This long connection with the north-west of India has left an indelible mark upon the character of the Buddhist and Hindu architecture of the valley. The early Buddhist religious edifices of Kashmir have practically the same plan, and probably had the same elevation, as the contemporary Buddhist buildings of Gandhara. There was, however, a considerable difference in the materials used and in the modes of decoration. At Ushkar, for instance, the abundance of local quarries ensured a plentiful supply of stone chips, which the builders turned to excellent advantage. At Harwan[5], on the other hand, the most easily available building materials are the round boulders and pebbles brought down by the Dachigam Nala. Here accordingly we find the chip-masonry of Ushkar replaced by walls built of small pebbles (The endeavour in each case seems to have been to employ building materials which were as small in size as possible.

SHANKARACHARYA TEMPLE

The most conspicuous monument that attrcta the attention of the visiter on reaching srinager the ancient temple on the crust of the sankaracharya hill standing 305 m above the plan the temple rests on the solid rock and consists of an octagonal basement of 13 layer of stone 20 feet height[6], on which is supported a square building on each of the four sides are two projections which terminate in pedimenet and a gable, the leter interesting the main roof half way of its slope.

The body of the temple is surrounded by a terrace enclosed by a stone wall or a parapet 31/2 ft high. This in fallowing the outline of the basement is preserves its octagonal shape. The terrace surrounding the temple is reached by the three flights of stone steps numbering 6, 7 & 18. The last being encased between two walls from the terrace another flight of 10 steps leads to door of the temple. The interior is a chamber, circular in plan with a basin containing lingam its general shape is that of a cone, with four sides formed by the rectangular adjustment of gable shaped salable opt masonry.

---

6. Bangroo Virender, Ancient Temples of Kashmir, vol, i p.p-37

7. Bamzai, P.N.K, Cultural and Political History of Kashmir, vol.i, p.p. 320

The cone which is about 20 ft n height, with a proportionate base rests upon an octagonal raised platform. Which is about 5 ft above the terrace? The circumference of the platform is about the 100 ft.

The interior of the temple is 14 ft in diameter the ceiling is flat and 10 ft high the walls which are 7 ft thick, are covered with white plaster composed of the gypsum and the roof is supported by 4 octagonal lime stone pillars. The whole of the building is of stone which is laid throughout in horizontal; courses, no cement is gave been appearing to have been used[7].

SHANKARACHARYA TEMPLE, SRINAGAR

SHIVA TEMPE, LODUV

Three miles and a half above Pandrethan, the road branches off to the sulphur springs at Wuyan and the Khruv game preserves. The branch road skirts the foot of the hills, and after describing a wide sweep of nearly 10 miles, joins the main road at Barus[8]. The village of Loduv is situated on this road at a distance of 3 miles from the last-mentioned place. It contains two temples, the larger one of which stands in the middle of a shallow tank of water which is fed by a spring in its north-east corner. The temple is a

8. Bamzai, P.N.K, Cultural and Political History of Kashmir, vol.i, p.p. 320
9. Walter Lawrence, The Valley of Kashmir, p.p.45
10. Kak. R.C, Ancient Monuments of Kashmir, p.p. 55

very simple structure 24' square externally. It differs from every other temple of Kashmir both in plan and in appearance. Internally the temple is circular with a diameter of 17' 6". In this respect it resembles the Sankaracharya temple on the Takht-i-Sulaiman hill. The wall surfaces are quite plain. At a height of nearly 10 feet from the ground level is a plain projecting string-course over which springs the domical ceiling. The dome was built of projecting courses of kanjur in lime, and must have been similar to the ceiling of the larger temples at Wangath. The holes and mortises in the walls seem to have been intended for scaffolding while the temple was under construction[9].

TEMPLE ARCHITECTURE UNDER KARKOTAS

The real patron & to some extent the founder of sophisticated Aryan style of Kashmir architecture was Lalitaditya who built the new city Parihaspura with the imposing temples & Chaityas, the famous Sun temple of Martand & the similar but picturesque temple of Wangath and possibly some temples in the Punjab at kaller, ketes and kaferkot (Bilot). In his constructions we notice a transformation achieved by the absorbtion of many new inspiration, ideas and techniques from the more developed civilization in India and countries to her north & west. Like so many compare builders Lalitaditya took artists from where ever he could obtain them and pride in mould different styles and techniques into a new imperial art bearing the impress on his own personality[10].

His principal minister, Cankuna, erected the great stupa at Parihaspura and other stupas at Pandrethan, decorated with sculptures in the Wei and T'ang Chinese art the great Chaityas of his which the foundation have been un earthed, fallows the Ghandhar style of architecture in its plan, and Kalhanas records the installations in it of a huge Buddha image moulded perhaps on the Bamiyan colossus.

The ruins of the two famous temples Parihasakesava and Mukta kesava at Parihaspora show vast enclosed courts surmounted by chapels bigger in scale than the one at Narasthan- a plan on which a temple at Martand was also built.

SUN TEMPLE, MARTAND

The temple of Martand is situated at a distance of 5 miles from the town of Anantnag. Being on the top of a Lofty plateau, at whose feet stretch the

---

11. this chapter was first published in article from the Rupam of Calcutta
Issues and Problems in the Sociology of Jammu & Kashmir

broad verdant plains of Kashmir. The temple of the Sun, as Martand originally was, commands a superb view, such as the eye rarely lights upon. It is this beauty of situation that contributes so largely to the sense of grandeur with which the sight of these ruins always inspires even the most unimaginative visitors[11].

Like most mediaeval temples of Kashmir, Martand consists of a courtyard with the principal shrine in the middle and a colonnaded peristyle. The latter is 220 feet long by 142 feet broad and contains eighty-four fluted columns facing the courtyard. The peristyle is externally plain, except on the west side, which originally had a row of columns similar to that of the Awantipora temples[12]. The entrance, or gateway, stands in the middle of the western side of the quadrangle, and is of the same width as the temple itself. Outwardly the Martand gateway resembles the temple itself in the disposition of its parts and in the decoration of its pediments and pilasters. This was no doubt closed with a wooden door.

On each flank of the gateway the pediment was supported by massive fluted pillars, 17.5 feet in height, or 8 feet higher than those in the quadrangle. The roof was no doubt pyramidal; for a portion of the sloping moldings of its pediment was still to be seen on one side." The walls of the gateway are profusely decorated internally and externally. Most of the pedimented niches contained single standing figures of gods; occasionally they also contained an amorous group similar to those at Avantipur. The rectangular panels contained sitting groups, floral scrolls, pairs of geese, etc. The temple proper "is 63 feet in length by 36 feet in width at the eastern end and only 27 feet in width at the western or entrance end. the middle one, called antarala or 'mid temple,' corresponding to the promos of the Greeks, is 18 feet by 4 inches; and the innermost, named garbhagriha, or 'womb of the edifice,' the naos of the Greeks and the cella of the Romans, is 18 feet 5 inches by 13 feet 10 inches[13].

Among the images carved on the walls of the antarala and the antechamber, we notice on the left wall of the former a well executed image of the river-goddess Ganga, standing upon her vehicle, the crocodile, which is looking up towards her. A female attendant on her right holds an umbrella over her head, and a chart-bearer is on her left. She holds her usual emblems, a water pot in her left hand and the stalk of a lotus flower in her right. Most of the hands of the images are unfortunately broken and

---

12. Cole, H, Kashmir Monuments. P.p.56

14. Kak, R.C, Ancient Monuments of Kashmir, p.p.34

Issues and Problems in the Sociology of Jammu & Kashmir

weather-worn, and the emblems they hold can no longer be identified. Nor can the fourteen seated figures which occur on the walls of the antechamber below the cornice be identified with certainty. Twelve of them occur in the north and south walls - i.e., six on each, and two on the east wall. Of the two panels on the east wall, the one on the right seems to represent Aruna, the charioteer of Surya, holding the reins of his seven horses. The pilasters of the great trefoil arch of the antechamber contain images which cannot yet be identified." " The chapels to the north and south of the antechamber each contain two niches 5' 9" by 4' internally, which face to the east and west respectively, possibly an allusion to the rising and setting of the sun[14]. The roof seems to have been of the pyramidal type common in the temples of Kashmir.

The peristyle is the largest example of its kind in Kashmir. In the middle of its larger sides there are a pair of large fluted pillars, 13' in height and 8 3/4' apart, somewhat advanced beyond the line of the other cells. "The quadrangle itself contained seventy round, fluted pillars, and ten square parallel pillars which with the four pillars of the central porches make up the number of 84 that was sacred to the sun. Of these about one-half, all more or less imperfect, now remains standing. . . . Each pillar was 9 1/2' in height, and 21 1/2" in diameter, with an intercolumniation of 6' 9 1/2".... The imposts (behind) were surmounted by human-headed birds facing each other, and a smaller bird, looking to the front, ornamented the horizontal moldings of the pediments [15].

SHIVA TEMPLE, 'WANGATH'

The Srinagar-Sonamarg high road branches off at Wusan to the mountain village of Wangath and the long and narrow glen known to sportsmen by the name of Wangath Nala. The dense dark green forests of pine and fir which clothe the steep and in some places almost vertical hillsides are favorite haunts of the bear in early autumn, when maize begins to ripen. An uphill trudge of eight or nine miles brings the jaded traveler to Narannag, the site of an interesting group of temples which are commonly known as the Wangath temples, though the village bearing the name "Wangath " is three miles distant. They are situated at the foot of the Butsher Mountain, whose extreme steepness and slipperiness have become proverbial, arld have made it the terror and despair of Gangabal pilgrims[16].

Wangath comprises six temples situated within an enclosure wall. Judging by their positions, as they are by no means symmetrically disposed

---

16. Marshal, Sir John, Note on Archaeoligical work in Kashmir, p.p-65
17. Dutt, J C, Kings of Kashmir, Vol.iii. p.p.67

in relation to one another, and by the difference in their architectural details, it is probable that the various structures were built at different dates.

(1) The principal temple is a square of 25', and, except in a few particulars, does not differ from other temples of Kashmir. The first point of departure from the usual style is the entrances. We have seen the temples of the vimana type, which have all the four sides open. But this one has two entrances opposite each other in the north-east and south-west sides. The second distinction is its domed ceiling, though there is no doubt that externally the roof was pyramidal. A large quantity of lime has been used in the masonry of the temple. The ceiling is built of circular courses of kanjur stone, and is crowned at the apex by a full-blown lotus. The dome springs from four large corner stones, which cut off the angles formed by the walls. On two sides of the string-course upon which the dome rests are eight rectangular slots (four on each side), which seem to have been intended to hold the rafters of a canopy over the image. The interior measures 17' square. In the centre of the floor is a square space which is unpaved. It marks the site of the pedestal of the image. The mortises of the tenons of the doors can still be seen in both entrances[17]. This temple has been identified by Sir Aurel Stein with the Jyeshthega temple of Lalitaditya.

SHIVA TEMPLE BUNIAR

The Buniar is a village in district Baramulla near about 8 miles away. There is a temple situated on the Jhelum Valley road, two miles above Rampur. It is by far the best preserved of all the larger Kashmir temples. It was built in the 9th to 10th century A.D[18]. The gateway is a double-chambered structure faced on each open side by a trefoil arch surmounted by a steep pediment. The lintels of the closed arches are supported on pairs of columns which were originally fluted, though the weather has now left no trace of flutes. They have a double capital, the upper one being volute on all four sides. The walls are externally surmounted by a cornice of kirti-mukhas, alternating with miniature trefoiled niches.

The flights of steps-on the eastern and western sides respectively afford entrance to and exit from the entrance chamber. The one on the roadside is buried underground, but the inner stair has been excavated. It consists of seven steps flanked by sloping rails and upright side walls. Between this stair and the temple is a small stone platform which formed the lower most course of the stepped base of a column (most probably a Garudadhvaja).

The temple itself stands on a double base, which is in every respect similar to other structures of its kind in Kashmir. A lofty trefoil arch,

---

18. Bangroo Virender, Temples in Kashmir, p.p.78
19. Walter Sir Lawerance. The valley of Kashmir. .p. 54

standing upon advanced pilasters and enclosing a rectangular entrance originally surmounted by an ornamental trefoil and steep pediment, gives access to the sanctum. The jambs of the entrance are adorned with half-engaged columns. The interior is a square of 14 feet. The pedestal of the image is placed on a broad platform. The original image, which seems to have been of Vishnu, is now replaced by small Siva-lingas originally brought from the bed of the river Narbada. The walls are covered with a coat of modern whitewash.. It was, no doubt, similar to the ceilings of the larger temples at Wangath. Externally the only decorations are the trefoils of the recesses, their pediments, and the cornice of kirtimukhas and miniature trefoils from which the roof sprang.

Temple Architecture under Utpalas and Loharas

Avantivarman, who ascended to the throne of Kashmir in the latter half of the 9th century, ushered in another memorable era of architecture. He built a group of temples at Avantipur, a township eighteen miles from Srinagar, among which that of Avantiswami[19], dedicated to Vishnu, still survives in part. It has been said that whereas the Martand temple is the expression of a "sudden glory", the Avantiswami temple shows greater maturity of experience and has therefore more sophistication and elegance. Graceful colonnades of pillars form an arcaded portico around the shrine and a monolithic pillar before the entrance bears a metal figure of Garuda, the king of birds and vehicle of Lord Vishnu. Motifs borrowed from many sources, both foreign and indigenous, appear in the decorative carving, but these have been tastefully integrated into an ordered system with a recognizable unity. Designs reminiscent of Buddhist stone carvers of the Ashokan age and of the craftsmen of the Pala school are frequent, and symbols traceable to Byzantium, ancient Persia and Syria are also found. The conspicuously angular aspect of this temple is derived from the wooden houses of the valley where accumulation of heavy snow on roofs is prevented by their sloping character.

Two Shiva temples built at Pattan in the 10th century A.D., during the reign of Shankaravarman reveal that although the traditional mode established at Martand was still being followed two centuries later, the masonry tended to become more monolithic. The precision and skill with which the moldings are chiseled out of a huge stone is truly amazing.

Avantisvara Temple, Avantipura

The village of Avantipur, situated at a distance of 18 miles from Srinagar on the Anantnag cart-road, represents the town of Avantipura, founded by Avantivarman, who reigned from A.D. 855 to 883. Its chief interest centres in two magnificent temples with which its founder

---

20. Marshal, Sir John, Note on Archeological work on Kashmir, p.p,55

embellished it. The first and larger is the temple of S'iva-Avantisvara, whose massive walls rise in forlorn grandeur outside the village of Jaubror, half a mile below Avantipur[20]. The gateway is in the middle of this wall, and is divided into two chambers by a cross wall. Its walls are not decorated with figure sculpture. The niches and the panels are quite plain.

The base on which the shrine in the centre of the court-yard stands is 57 feet 4 inches square and 10 feet high. To each of its corners was attached a platform about 16' square, which must originally have supported a small subsidiary shrine. It has a stair on each of its four sides like the temple of Pandrethan. The stairs have a width of 28.5 feet, and are supported on either side by flank walls 17.5 feet in length. The sanctum has been reduced to a "confused mass of ruins[21]." The platforms seem to have originally been attached to the plinth of the temple at one point only, but afterwards they were completely joined with it by means of a connecting wall built of architectural fragments which had fallen from the temple. This arrangement can best be seen at the south-eastern corner of the base. The sole exterior decoration of the temple base, the only part of the building that exists, is a series of projecting facets, the larger of which were originally surmounted by plain rectangular capitals.

Shankaragaurisvera, Siva Temple Pattan

The Rajatarangini mentions the erection of three temples at Patan, which in ancient days was called S'ankarapurapattana[22], after the name of its founder, King S'ankaravarman (A.D. 883-902). Perhaps it would be well to remark here that vandalism of a serious kind had already begun in pre-Muslim times, as some of the materials used in the construction of these temples were removed from the older site of Parihasapura described above.

The three temples named by the Kashmir chronicle are (1) S'ankaragauris'vara, (2) Sugandhesa, and (3) Ratnavardhanesa. The first, identified with the larger temple near Patan, was built by the king himself, the second, which is the one nearer Srinagar, is named after Sugandha, his queen, and the third, of which no trace has so far been found, if we exclude the architectural fragments near the spring outside the dak bangalow, was built by Ratnavardhana, his minister. All three were dedicated to Siva.

Lower down is the larger temple built by the king himself .It is only an enlarged copy of the queen's temple. On account of the lack of proper facilities for drainage of rain water it has not been deemed advisable to excavate its courtyard. The peristyle, the temple-plinth, and a smaller shrine in the north-east corner, are therefore still underground. The rectangular

---

21. Bangroo Virender, Temples in Kashmir, p.p. 45
22. Kak R C, Ancient Monuments of Kashmir, p.p.76
23. Cunnigham, Journal of Asiatic Society of Bengal, p.p. 76

Issues and Problems in the Sociology of Jammu & Kashmir

path around the temple marks the position of the peristyle, tops of some columns of which are seen peeping out of the earth in the south-west corner. The square flower-bed with a projection on one side in the north-east corner of the courtyard coincides with the small shrine below. The square space in the middle of the eastern path marks the position of the entrance[23].

The temple itself is an imposing pile, though a great deal of its grandeur has been taken away by the concealment of its plinth. The cella is 17' square and the central stone of the floor measures 12' 6" by 10'. It has nine circular holes arranged in three rows. It is possible that these were mortices of tenons which held in position the pedestal of the idol. The left wall of the portico has a trefoiled niche which is divided into two panels. The lower and larger one contains a number of figures, of which the principal seems to be S'iva. Above it, in the upper foil, is the squatting figure of the elephant-headed god, Ganesa, whose presence here would conclusively prove, even if there were any doubt about it, that the temple was dedicated to Siva. The jambs of the recesses on the exterior of the temple have half-engaged columns which are decorated with well-executed geometrical and other patterns. Their capitals are surmounted by human-headed birds.

A few yards to the north of the Patan dak bangalow has recently been excavated an old baoli whose waters are confined in three rectangular reservoirs which are connected with each other. The one in the middle contains a miniature temple constructed originally of three stones .The top-stone is missing. It is 2' 8" square externally and is open on all four sides. The openings seem to have been closed originally with wooden doors. These little shrines belong to the time when the prosperity of the Hindus had waned, and they were not capable of devoting so much wealth to the glorification of their religion.

Shiva Temple Pandrethan

The small village of Pandrethan is situated 3 miles above Srinagar on the Anantnag cart-road. At present its only attraction, excepting the newly built military barracks, is the well-preserved mediaeval temple behind the willow grove on the left-hand side of the cart-road .The temple measures 17 feet 6 inches square externally, and belongs to the mandapa type - i.e., it is open on all the four sides. The unusually bold projection of the pilasters which support the pediments of the porches is "a great improvement upon the earlier stage, as the boldness of the projection and the retirement of the connecting walls afford a great and pleasing variety of light and shade which

---

24. Bamzai, PNK. Culturtal and Political History of Kashmir, vol i, p.p. 75

is altogether wanting in some parts of the more ancient buildings[24]." The roof is of the usual pyramidal type, but its monotony is relieved by an ornamental band of dentils which divides it horizontally into two storeys.

In the upper section of the pyramid are four trefoiled ventilation apertures which remind one forcibly of similar niches in the architecture of Gandhara. The interior of the cellar is plain, except for the ceiling, which is one of the best examples of carving on stone extant in Kashmir. It consists of nine stones arranged in three overlapping squares, each of which cuts off the angles of the square below it, and thus reduces the extent of the space to be covered. The twelve triangles so formed have been utilized for figure decoration. Each triangle in the lowest square contains a pair of flying Yakshas, facing each other and holding a garland in their hands, which falls in swags about their bodies and between their knees. The second group of triangles contains only four figures, each holding a disc in his right hand and a lotus stalk in his left. Underneath his right arm is seen the outstretched end of flying drapery. The uppermost set of triangles contains a similar group of flying figures. The whole is crowned by a square slab decorated with an exquisitely carved full-blown lotus within a beaded circle. The convention, by which the peculiarly graceful floating motion of the body, somewhat similar to that of a swimmer, is made to represent the flight of human figures without the appendage of wings, is noteworthy. The floor of the cella is paved with stone flags. In the centre is the depression about 7 feet square which must have held the pedestal of the image worshipped in the temple.

Cunningham, and after him Cowie, Cole, etc., believed that the temple was "Vishnu-meruvardhanasvami," built by Meruvardhana, the minister of Partha who flourished in the beginning of the tenth century A.D. He bases his identification on the statement of the Rajatarangini coupled with absence of other temples in Pandrethan. But this theory is considerably weakened by the presence, in the trefoiled niche above the northern entrance, of a seated figure which is believed to be the Lakulis'a form of Siva, and by the internal arrangement of the floor of the cella which "can only admit of a Siva image." The Rajatarangini mentions in another passage the erection of the temple of S'iva-Rilhanesvara by Rilhana, the minister of Jayasimha, about the year A.D. 1135. There is nothing in the architectural style against the identification of our temple with Rilhana's foundation. Around this site a number of late Brahmanical images have been found.

---

25. Kak, R C, The Ancient Monuments of Kashmir, p.p-67

Siva Temple, Payar

Three miles farther, and situated at the foot of the Karewa on the opposite side of the rivulet, is the village of Payar[25], which contains a very elegant little temple. The name Payach, which has obtained currency through Vigne and Cunningham, is not known locally. The identification of the temple with the temple of Narendrasvami, built by Narendraditya circa A.D. 483-490, proposed by General Cunningham, is in keeping neither with the style of architecture according to which it could not be assigned to about the eleventh century A.D. nor with its dedication to Siva, as the name Narendrasvami would presuppose its dedication to Vishnu.

This temple, in spite of, or perhaps more correctly on account of, the feeble attempt that has been made to dismantle it - the top stone of the roof is still out of position - is by far the best preserved example of a mediaeval Kashmiri shrine. It is 8 feet square internally and 21 feet high, including the base, the chief moldings of which are a plain torus in the middle and a filleted torus on the top. The sanctum is open on all sides, but is reached only by a single flight of steps on the east side. The doorways are rectangular, and are surmounted by a trefoil arch, which in turn is enclosed by a pediment. The pilasters on which the pediments rest are surmounted by capitals bearing pairs of geese with long foliate tails, and the pilasters from which the trefoiled arch springs are crowned by recumbent bull capitals.

The bulls have scarves tied to their humps. The eastern trefoil itself encloses a relief, in which Siva is seen seated cross-legged on a throne under the canopy of an overhanging tree, surmounted by votaries, two of whom are seated, European fashion, with legs hanging down. On the north side the relief represents Bhairava, the terrible manifestation of Siva, pursuing a human being, who turns towards him in an attitude of supplication. Behind the Bhairava is a long elephant's trunk. On the west side is the very animated figure of six-armed dancing Siva. The upper two arms are raised aloft, holding the two ends of a scarf. The middle two hands are gesticulating, the lowest left hand holds a flower and the right the trident, the special emblem of S'iva. In the left lower corner of the group is a musician playing on a vina (lute); on the right is another beating a drum in accompaniment.

The superstructure is built of ten stones only. "In the interior the walls are plain, but the roof is hollowed out into a hemispherical dome of which the centre is decorated by an expanded lotus flower. The lower edge of the dome is ornamented by three straight-edged fillets and by a beaded circle. The spandrels are filled by single undraped and winged figures (of rather

---

26. Stein M A, Rajatarngini, trans, vol.i.p.p.330

spirited execution), who with outstretched arms and legs appear to be supporting the roof. They are probably Yakhshas. The dome itself rests upon the cornice, which is formed of six plain straight-lined mouldings." The ceiling of the Pandrethan temple is a copy of this on a larger scale. The cult image of the temple is a giva-linga, which has an octagonal base.

Temple construction techniques

The temple builders of Kashmir were way ahead of their contemporaries of the plains and peninsular India. The 8th century temples of Kashmir were constructed of evenly dressed ashlar masonry. Built of mammoth boulders, the joints were put together with lime mortar, which is seen at Wangat, and also steel dowels, used in the Martand temples. These engineering developments were in vogue in the neighboring western region of Kashmir. These refined techniques could not stand up the rigorous climate of the region and human vandalism and only a few of the vast number of temples, described so eloquently by Kalhana in Rajtarangni, have survived[26].

---

27. op. cit, 88

REFERENCES

1. Agarwal, J. C, *The History Of Ancient Kashmir*, edition, 2006.
2. Agarwal, R. C, *Kashmir and its Monumental Glory*. Published, Delhi, 1996.
3. Alberuni, *India*. Translated by E. Sachau.
4. Bangroo Virendra, *The History of Kashmir*. In edition 1995.
5. Beal, Samuel, Life *of Hiuen Tsiang*.
6. Buhler, Georg, Report *of a tour in search of M.S.S. F.B.B.R.A.S*
7. Cole, Lietutenant, H, *Kashmir Monuments*. Published & re-edition 1991.
8. Cowie, Rev. W.G, Notes *on some of the temples of Kashmir in the f.A.S.B. 1866*
9. Cunningham, Sir Alexander, *Essay on the arian Order of Architecture in the f.A.S.B. 1848*.
10. Cunningham, Sir Alexander, *Ancient Geography of India*. Published under Delhi in 1965.
11. Drew, F, *Jammu and Kashmir Terrioteries*. Re-edition, 1998.
12. Dutt, J. C, *Kings of Kashmir*, Vol.iii
13. Elephinstone, Mountstuart, *History of india*.
14. Fergusson, James, *History of India and Eastern Architecture*.
15. Ferishta, *History of India*. Translated by Colonel Briggs.
16. Haig, Colonel. *The Sultans of Kashmir*, 1918.
17. Kapur M. L, *The History of Kashmir*, Kashmir, 1998.
18. Lawerance, Sir Walter, *The Valley of Kashmir*.
19. Marshall, Sir Joh,. *Note on Archeological Work in Kashmir*, Delhi, 1981.
20. Nicholls, J.H, *Mughal Gardens of Kashmir*. Jammu, 1991.
21. Nicholls, J.H, *Muhammadan Architecture of Kashmir*. A.S.R. 1906-07.
22. Panikkar, K, *Gulab Singh*. Delhi, re-edition, 1997.
23. Sahni, daya Ram, R. B, *Pre-Muhammadan Monuments of Kashmir*, in the A.S.R. for 1915-16. Avantipur temples.
24. Sharma S K & S R Bakshi, *Kashmir Encyclopedia*.
25. Singh, Luckvinder, Sodhi, *The History of Ancient Kashmir*, edition 2002.
26. Suresh K. Sharma, *Kashmir Society and Culture, S R Bakshi*, edition, 2005.
27. Si-yu-ki, *The Buddhist Records of the western World*. Translated by Beal.
28. Smith, V. A, *Early History of India*. Bombay, 1961.
29. Stein, Sir Aurel , *Notes on the Rajtarngini*. Vol.i.
30. Watters, Thomas, *On Yuan Chwang's Travels in India*.

WEBLIOGRAPHY

1-http://koausa.org/Monuments/Introduction.html
2-http://koausa.org/monuments/chapter5.html
3-http://koausa.org/Monuments/Chapter6.html
4-http://www.koausa.org/geography/chapter1.4.html
5-http://www.koausa.org/Monuments/Chapter5.html
6-http://www.peacekashmir.org/jammu-kashmir/geography.htm
7-http://www.docstoc.com/docs/53887385/Geography-of-Jammu-

Kashmir-State
8-http://ikashmir.net/geography/index.html

CHAPTER- XI

DISABLED CHILDREN: CONCEPT, PROBLEMS AND CHALLENGES

SPECIAL REFERENCE TO JAMMU AND KASHMIR

RAVI KUMAR

Introduction

Ever since the dawn of civilization, human society has been faced with the problem of disability. Children with defects were not cared for in prehistoric societies. Defects like mental illness in the good old days were considered the results of some kind of sin. The treatment meted out to them varied from age to age, civilization to civilization and culture to culture. The Spartans destroyed them by throwing them down, tumbling the mountain precipices; the Egyptian Pharaohs hanged their blind slaves from the branches of trees. The physicians and the scholars in ancient Greek and Roman societies however, made some efforts to treat and preserve the lives of the physically challenged and provided asylums. The renaissance brought a small change in earlier attitude. This was the state of affairs until the late eighteenth century and early nineteenth century.

Situation in India was not better. In ancient India, however, during the golden rule of Ashoka the disabled received humane treatment. The first attempt at educating the disabled children were made in the last two decades of the 19th century with the establishment of First School for hearing impaired in Mumbai in 1885, followed by the First school for the visually impaired in Amritsar in 1887. In India, according to the census 2001, there are 2.19 thousand people with disability who constitute 2.13 percent of the total population. Out of 21,906,769 people with disabilities, 12,605,635 are males and 9,301,134 are females and this includes persons with visual, hearing, speech, locomotors and mental disabilities. In contrast, the National Sample Survey Organization (NSSO) estimated that the number of persons with disabilities in India is 1.8 percent of the Indian population. The difference in the estimates of the census and NSSO for different types of disabilities can be explained by the lack of universal definition. The prevalence of disability is marginally higher among males than among females throughout the world.

The union government has responded positively to this problem with such a magnitude. It legislated the 'Persons with Disability Act' in 1995 which aimed at:

- To spell out the responsibility of the state towards the prevention of disability, protection rights, provision of medical care, education, empowerment and rehabilitation of persons with disability.
- To create barrier free environment for persons with disability.
- To remove any type of discrimination with disabled persons.
- To counteract any situation of abuse and exploitation of persons with disability.
- To lay down strategies for comprehensive development of programmes and services and equalization of opportunities for disabled persons.
- To make special provisions for the integration of disabled persons into the social mainstream

To cater to the needs of such a high disabled population, at present, there are more than 243 schools for visually impaired, 478 for hearing impaired and 604 for mentally retarded children. Vocational Rehabilitation Centre (VCR) has been set up. National Institutes have started functioning. A 3% job reservation has been brought in and a special employment exchange has been set up. National Awards, tax concessions, self employment schemes, and sheltered workshops are available for the disabled. Establishment of District Rehabilitation centre (DRC), Community Based Rehabilitation (CBR), Regional Research Training Centre (RRTC), National Information Centre for Disabled and Rehabilitation (NICDR) are among the other efforts made by the Govt. for the welfare of the disabled.

Jammu and Kashmir also faces the problem of disability in acute form. Its occurrence in the state has reached an alarming level as the percentage of disabled population is much higher than the national average. According to 2001 census record of Jammu and Kashmir, the state had more than 300 thousand disabled persons. The figure of disability in the state in 2011 according to experts must have doubled. The reason cited for the high increase includes more than the normal increase due to hilly nature of the state and higher rate of disability due to armed conflict in last two decades. The blind, movement and mental disability were more prevalent in proportion than speech and hearing disability. Census figures revealed that majority of the disabled (i.e. about 56% of the total) were illiterate in comparison to minority of literate (i.e. about 44% of the total) in the year 2001. Again majority of disabled belonged to lower and middle classes, minority of them were from upper and elite. A comparative view of census 2001 revealed the higher rates of disability in Jammu and Kashmir in comparison with the national average and the north states' rates. Thus while the national level disability percentage in 2001 was 2.12 percent, the Jammu and Kashmir had 3.00 percent. The north states of Punjab, Himachal Pradesh and Chandigarh which share the hilly character with Jammu and Kashmir had disability rates of 1.7 percent, 2.56 percent, and 1.72 percent respectively in the same year. Jammu and Kashmir had the highest rate of disability which can be explained in terms of the hilly topography of the state and continuing armed conflict situation for the last twenty three years.

Table 1.1
Table Showing the District Wise Rate of Disability in Jammu and Kashmir

District	Disability Rate (in percent)
Baramulla	3.86
Srinagar	2.81
Budgam	2.58
Pulwama	2.53
Anantnag	2.63
Leh	2.31
Kargil	2.51
Doda	3.29
Udhampur	3.00
Poonch	3.80
Rajouri	3.15
Jammu	3.02
Kathua	2.30
Kupwara	3.25

Source: **Census, 2001**

Statistics clearly shows that four particular frontier districts of Baramulla, Poonch, Kupwara and Rajouri had high rates of disability against non frontier districts of the state. This was also because of the context of armed conflict in the state.

With such prevailing state of affairs in the state, one can imagine the problems that the children who are physically challenged must be facing. The problem of these children lies not only in the limitations that they have but also in their feeling a 'sense of inadequacy' and 'insecurity' due to the attitude of rejection, isolation, and even ridicule by others around them. These children, at times, can show negative and aggressive behavior because of certain bodily disorders such as anemia, blood sugar, hormone imbalance or neurological disorders which contribute to their emotional upsetting. Due to this, they find it difficult to adjust with their environment and develop certain personality disorders like lack of confidence, inferiority complex and often show tantrums to attract the attention of others. This calls for an appropriate environment within their homes and institutional care as per their requirements viz. depending upon the type of disability they are suffering from. Parents are vitally important throughout a child's life as a source of love and security, as teachers and as role models. But they are apparently important in the earliest years of child's life. These years are crucial for developing the emotional, social, physical, language and thinking skills, a child need throughout his or her life. But unfortunately, because of faulty parenting style, the young child become extremely miserable and it paves the way for different neurotic and other disorders among children which in turn pave the way for disabilities among children. Not only child suffers from this problem throughout his or her life but also the family of the child suffers at the same time.

Living with disabled children can have profound effect on the entire family- parents, siblings and extended family members. It is unique shared experience for the family and can affect all aspects of family functioning, the time, the financial costs, physical and emotional demands are much more needed for the family to support disabled children. The care for such children put an additional financial burden on the family who, often face issue of stigma and have to deal with the emotional stresses related to parenting such children. Parents of such children often face the problem of getting adequate care as there is lack of institutional care in our society.

The state government's response to the problem of disability has not been so active and positive. Except emphasizing implementation of the central act, its total response may be characterized as apathetic. Even the concerned government department has failed to collect basic data about disabled persons in Jammu and Kashmir. In this context, even the Governor of the state has to emphasis on the Social Welfare Department to conduct tehsil wise survey of disabled persons in the state. There are some centrally sponsored schemes with some minimum benefits to the disabled persons. But at the same time, these are neither fully functional nor the entire disabled community has been covered. These facilities also do not have expert personnel, modern medical technology and other resources.

There are some organization like 'Shafaqat Special School for Mentally Challenged and Multiple Disability' based in Srinagar which was founded in 1995 that is providing rehabilitation treatment to about 650 disabled children in the field of physiotherapy, occupational, audiology, speech therapy, recreational therapy, computer therapy, development therapy, special education and social activities. But there is a lack of such institutions in other regions. A handful of them are functioning in other regions like 'Sahara' school for the rehabilitation of physically and mentally challenged children in Jammu and 'Asha' school in Udhampur district.

The present study was conducted at Asha School in Udhampur district to get insights into the incidence of disability of children in the state of J&K and particularly in Udhampur district. The study has focused on the total institutional care available for children with special needs. Difficulties faced by parents in the form of emotional stress, stigma and financial burden have also been studied.

Conceptual Understanding of Disability

The disability has been conceptualized both medically as well as socially. It is important to conceptualize disability socially because the problems of disabled people have been explained historically in terms of divine punishment, karma or moral failing. Disabled find themselves isolated, stigmatized and excluded because of the inadequate social setup, improper public and personal transports, unsuitable attitude towards them, lack of working facilities and vocational training etc.

Throughout centuries, the disabled have been oppressed, marginalized and stigmatized in almost all societies. They have been excluded from every aspect of social life and constitute a section of population, which is most backward, least served and neglected. To put it simply, the person with disabilities represent the 'poorest of the poor' and 'weakest of the weak', which have been socially, educationally, economically and politically excluded. The degree of disability problem in society varies from country to country. The problem of disability is acute in both developed and developing countries. While in developed countries, industrial workers and old persons are directly and primarily affected by disability, in developing countries disability is mainly caused by poverty, malnutrition, and un-hygienic situations, affecting mostly children and poverty stricken population. However, two trends are more or less similar in both societies, firstly wars, industrialization, disease, accidents and other emerging social problems in both the societies (Singh & Kachhap, 2008).

In many parts of the world, war is a major cause of impairment. Consequently, world peace has become a disability issue. For example, at least 2,000 people are killed or injured every month by landmines in more than seventy countries around the world. Wars and political upheaval have a variety of impacts on people's lives (Priestly, 2001). Secondly, the lack of comprehensive policies concerning the prevention of disability and the rehabilitation of disabled persons suggests that most of them are dependent on the assistance provided by their families as well as public, thus imposing additional burdens on the families and societies (Karna, 1999).

The phenomenon of disability does not exist outside the periphery of our social system. It is a part of our social life as it is socially constructed. In other words, the physical, mental or intellectual disability is not an attribute of an individual but a complex accumulation of conditions, activities and relationships. We can get deeper insights into the concept of disability by relating it with various sociological perspectives.

Types of Disabilities

Disability means something that incapacities or disqualifies. These are certain problems in defining disability. The complexity of the concept of disability is undisputed and various factors are associated with the problems of definition. A worker may suffer from chronic bronchitis or may have lost a limb, a young girl may have facial disfigurement or breast cancer, and a person may be a victim of leprosy with whom no one would probably like to mix up because of pre existing social stigma. These are only a few examples that point to the complexity of the concept of disability. Disability conditions may be found among the children or adults everywhere in the world. they may be victim severely mentally impaired, deficient or retarded or handicapped, some children may be slow learners; while others may have speech or language defects, they may be partially or totally deaf or blind or partially sighted still some may be orthopedically handicapped who cannot move about normally. Individuals may be affected with various combinations of such conditions, accidents, infectious disease and other conditions. Different types of disabilities along with possible causes may be conveniently grouped below;

Table 1.2
Table Showing the Type of Disability and Classification with Causes

Type of disability	Classification	Causes
Impaired vision	Total blindness Partial blindness	Infectious diseases, injuries, poisoning, tumours, pre-natal influences
Auditory impairment	Deafness Hard of hearing	Pre-natal influences, injuries, mental retardation, physical handicap
Speech defects	Defects of articulation Defects of phonation Defects of fluency Language dysfunctions	Organic, psychogenic, functional
Orthopaedic	Injured limbs	Post polio residual, paralysis,

Issues and Problems in the Sociology of Jammu & Kashmir

handicap	Awkward movements of muscles	Cerebral palsy, tuberculosis
Brain injury	Cerebral palsies Mental retardation Sensory defects	Circulatory disturbances, disturbed metabolism, growth and nutrition, brain trauma, drug/poison intoxication, epilepsy, infections, miscellaneous causes
Mental retardation	Profound Sever Moderate Mild	Chromosomal aberrations and other complexities, infections during pregnancy, medical complications, environmental derivation, familial mental retardation, unknown causes

Source: **Sen, 1988**

Consequences: Psychological and Physical

Whatever may the form of disability, it is always has some social consequences. Physique is supposed to be one of the very crucial factors in the formation of personality; it is thus imperative that disability is almost invariably associated with the psychological problem. if normal variation in physique such being strong or a weak, tall or short, handsome or ugly are important factors in peer group formation, evidently pathological variation in the form of physical disability are quite potent factors in forming the negative body image of an individual. It is very difficult to estimate the incidence and prevalence of various types of disabilities among the Indian population because of some inherent problems. The detection of disability for that matter is not easy in any part of the world, particularly because of the problem of accurate definition.

References

Colin Barnes and Geof Mercer. (2010) *Exploring Disability- Second Edition.* Cambridge: Polity Press.

Despouy, Leandro. (1993), *Human Rights and Disabled Persons* (New York; United Nations), UN Publication.

French, Sally. (1994), *On Equal Term: Working with Disabled People* (Oxford: Butterworth Heinemann).

Insa, Klasing (2007). *Disability and Social Exclusion in India*: Rawat Publications.

Karna, G. N. (2001).*Disability Studies in India:* Gyan Publishing House.

Lang, Raymond. (1998), *A critique of the disability movement, Asia Pacific Disability Rehabilitation Journal,* 9 (1), pp. 4-8.

Oliver, Michael. (1983), *Social Work with Disabled People,* The Macmillan Press Ltd, London.

Oliver, Michael. (1990), *The Politics of Disablement,* The Macmillan Press Ltd, Basingstoke.

Priestley, Mark. (2001), *Disability and the Life Course: Global Perspective,* Cambridge University Press.

Sen, Anima. (1988). *Psycho-Social Integration of The Handicapped*: Mittal Publications.

Singh, Sudhir K.R. & Kachhap, A. (2008), *Disability, Citizenship and Exclusion,* Anamika Publishers.

CHAPTER- XII

SOCIOLOGICAL IMPLICATIONS OF DEVELOPMENT PROJECTS

CASE STUDY OF DUL AND HASTI PROJECT IN KISHTWAR, JAMMU AND KASHMIR INDIA

SUDESH KUMAR

INTRODUCTION

Development stands for economic efficiency, social and moral decency of achieving certain basic qualities for a society and ensuring a decent livelihood for all. No doubt, development is the need and establishment of infrastructure projects is a necessity, but development is not considered merely an improvement in material conditions and the standard of living of people of a society. It also includes improvement in human index in terms of life expectancy, infant mortality, adult illiteracy and social condition of people. Development has different meaning for different disciplines, for the economist development is an increase in the growth rate on per capita income, for a politician it is the acquisition of some symbols of modernization and progress, for administrator, it is achieving the target of social planning and for a social anthropologist it is the enhancement of the quality of life or standard of living or satisfactions of the basic needs, aspiration level and happiness (Dube, 1988).

In newly independent India, big dams, power centers, factories and industrial units came to symbolize the magnanimous presence of the state and its will to build a prosperous and a modern India. Dams were the official solution to generating water resources for industries, irrigation and harnessing energy. The focus was on increasing agricultural production and generating hydropower to fuel industrial production. Interestingly, despite the crores of rupees spent on building large dams, most of India survives by exploiting ground water. Surface water or rivers cater to less than 10% of the water requirements in the country. In the post-independence period, India has been grappling with the problem of fast economic development through the implementation of numerous projects like dams, industries, airport, railways and roads. For this purpose large area of land has been acquired which has been resulted in the displacement of millions of people without proper concern for the resettlement and rehabilitation. Most of the development victims belong to the poor sections of the society like dalits, tribal, women and other backward classes (Murickan 2003).

In the state of Jammu and Kashmir (J&K), there are various development resources that exist but due to unavoidable circumstances, state can't exploit these resources effectively. Slowly and gradually J&K government took up the cause of development with the help of central government of India. On April, 1983 Prime Minister of India, laid the foundation of 390 MW Hydro-Electric project, to be built on the swift flowing Chenab River in Kishtwar District. Initially it was planned that 30 meter high concrete dam will be constructed across the mighty Chenab near Dul village 14 km away from Kishtwar on Paddar road. A tunnel of 9.78 km has been bored across the Kishtwar bend. Its diameters is 7.3 meters at Hasti an underground power house constructed had 3 turbines with a capacity of generating 130 MW of power each has installed; it is one of the biggest power projects in India. The Dul Hasti project has been taken over by National hydro Power Cooperation (NHPC) of India. The Dul Hasti project provided power to the Northern Grid with beneficiary states being Jammu and Kashmir, Punjab, Haryana, Uttar Pradesh, Rajasthan, Delhi and Chandigarh. The present endeavour is an attempt to analyse the implications in terms of its negative and positive consequences of construction of Dul Hasti Project in Kisthwar District of Jammu and Kashmir.

The World Commission on Dams (2000) with its worldwide survey report agreed that dams have adversely affected many people and societies. Displaced persons suffer losses and experience traumas, sharing more in plains than in gains of development (Cernea, 1996). It has been estimated that the big dams alone have displaced some 30-40 million people. Displacement here refers to the forced migration. It occurs in at least two distinguishable forms, direct displacement and indirect displacement. Direct displacement refers to the people who are removed from their land for the construction of dams and their reservoirs and other infra-structure projects. Indirect displacement by development on the other hand refers to the displacement that is mediated by process not directly under the control of decision makers, such as market processes and environment degradation resulting from different interacting development activities. During the last 50 years, some 3300 big dams have been built, most of them have led to large – scale forced eviction of vulnerable groups. However there is no reliable official statistics on the number of people displaced by development projects. Official figures state that as many as 21 to 33 million persons are likely to have been displaced. Case studies indicate that most official figures are estimates e.g. by official count 1, 10000 persons were displaced by the Hirakud dam in Orissa, while research put them at 1, 80,000 (Patnaik 1996).

DEVELOPMENT OR DISASTER

In the name of development, national elites through the institution of the state and market and often in collaboration with foreign capital have appropriated natural resources land, water minerals and forest for conversion is to commodities. The circulation goods which this has brought forth, has taken place primarily among the elite. The elite have, therefore; through such pseudo developmental activities impoverished the earth of its natural resources. The earth's impoverishment has meant that communities who depend upon the natural base for sustenance have been deprived of their resources. This alienation cannot be described in terms of loss of material livelihood only; it is most profoundly the loss of culture autonomy, knowledge and power (Baviskar 1997). Thus no amount of compensation or rehabilitation can make good the same people who have been pushed off their lands, forests, and river banks, and their water taken away by the state for the supposed good of the state.

Furthermore the credibility of big dams projects is undermined by the fact that genuine needs of the people can be met in other ways, water can be provided for draught prone areas, much more quickly and cheaply and equitably with the use of small scales schemes, some using traditional techniques, some using new methods and some using a combination of both. Increasing the efficiency, supply and use water can hugely expand the availability of water without the need for new dams. A 15 meters barrage on densely populated flood plains could have much more devastating impact than a 100 meters dam in a deep valley. An example could be India's Farakka Barrage (less than 15 m in height), which has had a devastating impact on the ecology and economy of downstream Bangladesh. There are a number of different factors that have a bearing up on the impact of a dam and therefore it seems almost impossible that a standard could be laid down for the same (Udombana 2000). Dams are potent symbols of triumphant technology and progress. In the second half of the 20th century the numbers of large dams roar from 5000-45000. Many have failed to deliver the promised benefits of increased electricity and agricultural productivity.

Dam project in Kishtwar has provided many positive benefits to the people of the district; their educational level has also become high because NHPC provided them better educational facilities. People have also been benefitted due to better health facilities and transport facilities. But development also has its dysfunctions, due to the construction of dam it is seen that it leads to the destruction of environment with the construction of roads and other infrastructure activities create additional pressure on forest. Degraded catchments also result in erratic water flows resulting not only in dry season shortages but also a surplus during heavy rainfall and cloudbursts, threatening the surrounding people and also the safety of the dam. The degradation of the catchments also adversely affects the biodiversity and other ecological functions of the forest.

The present research has studied the Dul Hasti project located in Kishtwar in Jammu & Kashmir with reference to the consequences of development arising out of construction of dam. The project is an embodiment of interstate relationship and cooperation amongst the states of Punjab, Rajasthan, Delhi, Chandigarh, Himachal Pradesh, Uttar Pradesh, Uttaranchal, and Jammu and Kashmir. Thus the Dul Hasti project considered as an epitome of development has also led to the migration of people from one setting to another. With the construction of dam people of Kishtwar found new way of earning livelihood they have left behind their traditional jobs and have engaged in private jobs. Children belonging to the area are studying in Kendriya Vidyalya (Central School). There is also some visible effect on the lives of women due to increase in educational facilities.

Some women have also got employment in Dul Hasti Project and they are not dependent on their husbands any more for their day to day necessities. They have become economically independent. Better Hospital facilities have also raised the health level of the people of the area. Road connectivity with rest of the state has also enhanced the economic productivity of the area and people have opened their own shops along the national highway and near the project sites. This has resulted in people becoming economically well off and they have started earning well.

Due to migration it was also seen that women's role also gets enhanced. If only the male member of the family migrates the whole responsibility of the family left behind, comes on the women's shoulders. But if the whole family migrates, the responsibility of the family is shared by both male and female members. It is also seen that migration has bad impact on the lives of the small children because they find new environment and new friends and try to adapt themselves in new environment. In Kishtwar it was found that small children indulged in crime for example the children of migrated families were involved in theft cases, activities and their role in terrorist activities also surfaced.

DAM PROJECTS IN INDIA: FEW CASE STUDIES

Large dam construction has been an important and expensive undertaking for the Indian government. While dams have enhanced agricultural productivity in India, there is no evidence that they have been very cost effective, and they have significantly adverse distributional implications. The case of large dams suggests strongly that distributional implications of public policies should be central to any evaluation. Clearly, the case of large dams suggests the need to understand the institutions and power structures that led to the implementation of these projects.

SONEBHADRA PROJECT

There are eleven projects in Sonebhadra district of Uttar Pradesh, constructed over a span of 32 years (1960-1992). The Rihand dam project (1960) displaced about 10,000 families and compensation given at that time

Issues and Problems in the Sociology of Jammu & Kashmir

was 30 times of land revenue which came to around less than Rs.100 to a few hundred rupees. What happened to the ousts who include a large number of Scheduled Tribes and Scheduled Castes was really unimaginable. Some of the families belonging to the first displacement have been displaced five times in 32 years .The NTPC project at Shaktinagar Sonebhadra displaced many families and provided them with meager cash compensation besides plots which were in a very bad condition according to the reports available. In fact Nehru must have visualized that the temples of modern India would make some people untouchable by not allowing the benefits to reach them. Thus it is a revitalization movement of the elites to maintain their supremacy in the area by causing large scale exploitation of the under privileged people. In the early eighties Rihand Thermal Power Project was established which caused the large displacement in the area

The compensation package has been disastrous in all projects in Sonebhadra since all of them followed the Land Acquisition Act of 1894 which provides cash compensation to only those who have direct interest in the title. In Sonebhadra, the land settlement records are not in proper shape. Most of the people there are land less and there are many people who derive their sustenance from land without owing it directly or indirectly like the share croppers, or as services castes working through Jajmani system. According to Saksena and Sen (1998), 5 85% of the oustess were landless and only 11% of them got jobs. The displaced people were resettled as communities, with complete disregarded to their age- old social structure and social organisation.

HIRAKUD DAM

It is the longest dam in the world, which was completed after eight years of construction work that began in 1956. It irrigates 5, 40,000 acres of lands. The project submerged 29 villages and 112,038 acres of cultivated land and displaced 22144 families. In an interesting study Baboo (1992) find that the ousts found it very difficult to settle down in the first 15 years .Earlier, most of them had agricultural and allied occupations. In the heterogeneous rehabilitation colony of Kashipalli, adaptation was less painful because the people could get jobs in the industrial and urban sector as the colony was close to an urban industrial milieu. But the people in the homogenous colony of Kudapali had to be content with poor quality agricultural land that was allotted to them. In the first few years the people had to survive on forest foods, roots and leaves. People in another village (partly submerged foreshore village) could revive their past mainly because houses were not submerged and because they had access to non-agricultural income in the nearby urban centres. In Sapne, people suffered the most and the peasants became pauperized. Even after three decades, people did not feel at home. Baboo says that the compensation package was very poor and rehabilitation plan was completely unsatisfactory as the planners had little knowledge about rural life. The community life of the villagers got completely scattered and the oustess, even after 30 years of displacement, are not able to reconstruct their past social space. Besides, the cost benefit analysis of the dam indicates that it has failed in its major objectives like electricity, irrigation flood control and enhanced agricultural production. Baboo opines that the decreasing facilities from this dam could make the dependent population increasingly restless, insecure and frustrated about their future course of action.

THE UPPER KOLAB PROJECT

It is located Koraput district of Orissa, for which work began in 1976 and which was completed in 1985. It produces 95 megawatt of farm power and is irrigating 47,985 hectares of land in the area. It displaced 147 villages with 5366 families, the majority of whom were tribal .They are resettled in 11 colonies far away from their native villages. Patnaik's (1996) empirical account on them shows that as expected, the compensation package was very poor, particularly the cash transactions. The money was kept in a post office or bank and the procedure required the signature of two account holders to with draw money. The rehabilitation colonies were set up virtually in the waste land where the people had to fetch water from a distance of three kilometres. The oustees were shocked because they were displaced from daru (wood), pani (water) dumba (ancestor) and hundi (village deity). They can no more marry their father's sister's daughter because all the kins were scattered now. Under the situation, either they had to remain unmarried or had to marry some other person, the concept of basagarh (dormitory) completely disappeared. The institution of family, kinship, religion and economy, in short, the entire social structure had been completely devastated. Now it was only a piece meal approach to life while learning to live with hunger, perceived terror of the sahukar (money lender shopkeeper) and the curse of the God.

THE KOEL KARO PROJECT

It is located in the Jharkhand area of Bihar. It will submerge 256 villages partially and 135 wholly. About 1, 50,000 people among whom 90% are tribal are to be displaced, 30,000 acres of sanasdaris (burial places) are also to be submerged to produce 710 megawatt electricity. The project was conceived in 1954, but the planning Commission gave clearance in 1973 and allocated RS. 173 crores which escalated to Rs. 1700 crores by 1994. The life expectancy of the project is merely 20 years but the human cost involved is unimaginable. The tribals who live on about 54 wild plants, herbs, and shrubs as food, medicine and timber are bound to be distressed by their displacement.

Issues and Problems in the Sociology of Jammu & Kashmir

NARMADA CASE

The Sardar Sarovar project in Gujarat, which has worldwide attention, is a burning example of peoples' protest against the mindful developmental activity of the policy makers. The Narmada Bacho Aandolan an NGO is opposing the project. It has very strong grassroots support and has received, according to Baviskar (1997), a support- base which is multi-class, multi-ethnic and multi-culture in nature. According to her, the NGO is posing a serious challenge to the State. However on the Narmada issue there are other NGOs (for example, the Arch Vahini) whose views are radically different from Narmada Bachao Aandolan (Das, 1996). The Arch Vahini, along with other NGOs first rejected the resettlement package that was offered and then combined together to demand better resettlement packages. After having wrested what are regarded to be appropriate deals from the government, they agreed to be associated with the rehabilitation process.

DUL HASTI PROJECT

Dul Hasti project began in 1983, it is a hydroelectric project situated in Kishtwar, and Jammu & Kashmir in India built by NHPC.The power plant is built on the swift flowing Chenab River in the Kishtwar region. It is one of the major projects implemented in Kishtwar which was commissioned in April 2007. The project provides peaking power to the northern grid with the beneficiary states being Jammu & Kashmir, Punjab, Haryana, Uttar Pradesh, Uttarkhand, Rajasthan, Delhi, and Union territory of Chandigarh. In Dul Hasti project, hydroelectric power project comprises a diversion dam at Dul across the river Chenab and power house at Hasti. The Dul Hasti project has 106 m long head race tunnel with a drop of 235 m carries water to the underground power house.The power house accommodates three turbine sets, each coupled to 130 MW generations. The Dul Hasti project involves the installation of three – generation units of 130MW each in Kishtwar district. The annual generate 1,928 million units of electricity which will be sold to Jammu & Kashmir, Punjab, Delhi, Uttar Pradesh, Rajasthan, Chandigarh, and Uttaranchal. On the total power generation, one per cent free power is for local area development in addition to twelve per cent free power to the host state.

The Dul Hasti project has three units and each unit has 130 MW. The power situation in the state has been a key focus area for the government for decades Jammu & Kashmir required around 1900 MW per year, at peak demand of which about 1000 MW is available. In Kishtwar the River Chenab has a more than 2,000 MW capacity to generate hydro power project. That is why Kishtwar was chosen as the location for constructing hydroelectric project. The construction of Dul Hasti project required a 700 –members' strong work force in its operational state 500 people will be working every day. The project involved excavation of an 11 km tunnel through the mountain. The contract for the power generation project was first awarded to a French consortium at a price of $50 million, who almost immediately asked for an upward price revision. The site was intended to capitalize on the proximity to a large river systems capable of providing the water capacity needed to run a hydroelectric plant of Dul Hasti dimension.

COMPENSATION

Compensation is determined on the basis of the market value of the property. Market value consists not only of the land value but also other advantageous components including standing trees etc. The market value may be assessed according to the sale vicinity and the comparable benefits and advantages. Where agricultural land has to be acquired, the compensation should be based on the use of land including its potentially and nature of land. Sale instances of similar land with similar advantage could be considered as best evidence for valuation in the absence of which the market value could be determined in some ways. Under section 23 of the Act, the statuary compensation includes the damages and incidental expenses for the standing crops or trees existing at the time of taking possession. The percentage of compensation has varied from time to time and place to place. After passing of amended Act in 1984, the solarium has been fixed at 30 per cent of the market value of the property This amount is granted in lieu of the injury and distress caused to the feelings of the owners. The Act also provides for payment of additional market value on the compensation. For the first 12 months, the interest is at nine per cent from the date of award. For delays beyond 12 months from the declaration of the award, the rate of interest is 15 per cent. The owner ship of landed property is an essential condition before one could claim compensation. However, those who do not have property or those who are indirectly dependent on it could not claim compensation (Menezes, 1991).

LABOUR ISSUE IN DUL HASTI PROJECT

During Dul Hasti project, various issues related to the people involved in working in the project came up. One of such incident was the labor issue with Jai Prakash Company. People of Kishtwar protested against the Jai Prakash Company, which had hired the contractors for DHP. People were angry because JP Company provided jobs to the outsiders as outsiders were more educated and highly skilled than local people. The agitation was started in village Sangrambhata, during this agitation one person died and more than ten persons were injured in the police firing.

After a long agitation the company agreed to provide employment to the local people. All the jobs were provided on two bases, one through company and the other through local contractors, who hired the lab our for various construction activities. As per the office record about 1200 people took the benefit of jobs provided by JP Company. When the project was completed in 2007, JP Company terminated the services of 1200 local laborers from the company. This resulted into another agitation against the company. The people were actively participated in this agitation and their popular slogans were to block the road (Ghera bhandi), local politicians also joined the agitation against the JP Company. After one month of agitation, company agreed to give compensation to the aggrieved laborers and this pacified the labourers because they got nearly 2 to 6 lakh rupees. From this compensation some of them started their own business and some of them invested money in other areas.

REHABILITATION AND RESETTLEMENT POLICY BY NHPC IN 2007

When the Dul Hasti project was started in Kishtwar in 1983 there was no Rehabilitation and Resettlement (R&R) policy. And those people who had lost their land they were given compensation in terms of money and jobs. But with the passage of time, Rehabilitation and Resettlement (R&R) policy was started by NHPC in 2007. Rehabilitation and Resettlement policy focuses on a thorough understanding of the social, cultural, intellectual and economic background of the affected people and knowledge of good practices which would enable them in taking appropriate measures to reduce the distress of Project Affected Persons. NHPC aims at building a rapport with the project affected persons gain their confidence and take all necessary measures to improve the overall quality of life of those who gave their land, house and memories for the development of hydro projects.

Social impact assessment is a crucial tool and should be conducted in depth for assessing real situation in the field and understanding people's perception about the project. Rehabilitation and Resettlement further emphasizes that a change in mind set is required by the project proponent. The focus should not be on acquiring land but on providing benefits to the people, whose lands are required for the project and make them feel comfortable. NHPC believes that Rehabilitation and Resettlement package has to be marketed among the people. Misunderstanding by stakeholders due to miss communication or lack of communication from project developers, is the major cause of unrest in project areas leading to anti-project feeling.

For communication to be effective, it is emphasized that communication should penetrate at all levels and section of the society, instead of restricting it to some elites and influential families/persons in the affected area. Importance should be given to identification of skills of affected stakeholders. If that is done eligible Project affected Persons (PAPs) can be given requisite training for getting a job and can be helped to get absorbed.

Hence the rehabilitation and resettlement policy introduced by NHPC build a rapport between the public who are affected by the project and give them appropriate compensation so that they not feel any kind of problem. This is an important addition because most studies shows that the oustees have to wait for many years before they receive compensation amount. The provision that they should be paid compensation and resettled before their migration is a step in preventing this situation.

POSITIVE CONSEQUENCES

WATER SUPPLY FOR DOMESTIC AND INDUSTRIAL USE

Properly planned, designed and constructed and maintained dams contribute significantly toward fulfilling our water supply requirements. The primary source of fresh water supply is from precipitation. Throughout the world, the hydrologic cycle varies and is not predictable. Of the total precipitation, only 1/3 remains for runoff to our rivers, the rest is lost to infiltration and evaporation. Only about 36% of this runoff is available the rest is lost to infiltration and evaporation. Only about 36% of this runoff is available for use. To accommodate the variations in the hydrologic cycle, dams and reservoirs are needed to store water and then provide consistent yearly supply.

MEETING THE AGRICULTURAL DEMAND FOR FOOD SUPPLY

One of the biggest uses of water on a worldwide scale is agricultural irrigation. This will account for about 1147 liters per day per capita by the year 2000. Since the early1990s, less than 1/5 of the land suitable for agriculture in the world has been irrigated, and it has contributed about 1/3 of world food production. It is estimated that 80% of additional food production by the year 2025 will come from irrigated land. Most of the areas in need of irrigation are in arid zones, which represent a major portion of the developing countries. Even with the widespread measures to conserve water by improvements in irrigation technology, construction of more reservoir projects will be required.

FLOOD CONTROL

Dams and reservoirs can be effectively used to regulate river levels and flooding downstream of the dam by temporarily storing the flood volume and releasing it later. The most effective method of flood control is accomplished by a number of multipurpose dams strategically located in a river basin. The dams are operated by a specific water control plan for routing floods through the basin without damage. This not only eliminates flooding, but provides other benefits such as water supply, irrigation, and hydropower and water quality. Management plans are established by comprehensive planning for economic development and with public involvement. Flood control is a significant purpose for many of the existing dams and continues as a main purpose for some of the major Dams of the world currently under construction.

HYDROPOWER

The availability of energy is essential for the socio-economic development of a nation. It is advantageous to use energy that is clean, efficient, dependable and renewable. Hydropower meets all of these requirements. In countries, where a vast amount of development still lies ahead, good conditions often exist for renewable energy sources. The technically most advanced and economical source of renewable energy is hydropower. Less than 20% of the world's estimated feasible hydropower potential has been developed.

RECREATION

The attractiveness of reservoirs for tourism is often a significant benefit, in addition to the other purposes of a dam. This is very significant in areas where natural surface water is scarce or non-existent. Recreational benefits associated with lakes, such as boating, swimming, fishing, bird watching and nature walks, are taken into account early at the planning stage, along with other objectives achieve a balanced project. The operation of the dam and reservoir can enhance tourism.

DEVELOPMENT OF ROADS

With the commission of Dul Hasti project in Kishtwar, many rural areas have developed due to construction of roads. It is estimated that more than 20 villages have taken benefit due to Dul Hasti project. In Dool village NHPC constructed the dam and Hasti village constructed the power house. It is also found that before the Dul Hasti project rural people has faced a lot of problems such as lack of transport and lack of good roads. But after the project the local people got the benefits of infrastructural development and as a result their life style also changed. In Kishtwar there are some villages in which more development related activities were done because these villages were near the road side these villages are (Dool, Draba, Bhagna, Hanzala, Banjwar Hasti, Shalimar, Colony, etc.) For development of hydroelectric project located in the remote areas, infrastructural facilities like construction of bridges strengthening of existing roads, efficient and reliable tele-communication links, better road transport or air services etc.

CHANGES IN LIVING STYLE

Dul hasti project in Kishtwar has changed the living conditions of people. The people living in Kaccha houses have constructed Pucca houses. In Kishtwar district developmental project directly or indirectly has lead to the improvement in standard of living of local population. When the developmental project was taking place in Kishtwar, it had a direct or indirect impact on all aspects of life. Due to economic development people moved from one place to another place and constructed pucca houses .It has been found that those people who are permanent employees in NHPC (Dul Hasti project) they have undergone a greater change in their living standard as compared to other persons who are employees on contractual basis. Economic change that the people have experienced has brought change in the standard of living like as food habits, dress pattern and traditional culture of people has undergone change. Residential colonies are fully equipped with facilities for education, health and extra-curricular activities; they bring substantial changes for better living.

CHANGES IN ECONOMY

The development projects directly affect economy, because traditional kinds of activities are replaced by advanced activities and the resources are better utilized. For example with the completion of irrigation-cum power projects, more area received irrigation and other agricultural facilities. The outcome was an increase in agricultural produce. The people who were having low income on account of uncertainties of rain and inaccessibility of other agricultural inputs started generating high income.

It is found that Dul Hasti project directly affected the economy. Before the developmental project started, agriculture was the main source of income for earning their livelihood, some local people were also earning their livelihood through domesticated animals, small business and some depended upon the forest. But with the passage of time when the Dul Hasti project got established in Kishtwar then the local people under went some change in their economy, as many of the people were engaged in project, some in business and some moved outside the state for earning better livelihood. Some people also migrated from rural to urban areas in search of jobs. With the start of construction of work, the strength of NHPC staff and contractors and labor increased, thus the demand of consumption of daily needs such as foods grains, vegetables, milk, fruits, clothing, meat, and other requirements also increased which gave a boost to the business of the local business men.

CHANGES IN EMPLOYMENT PATTERN

In Kishtwar it is found that agriculture and small business were the main source of income. In Dool village it is found that mostly people were earning their livelihood through agriculture and cattle rearing. Developmental projects although result in the migration of people but at the same time they also create new jobs and opportunities. It is also found that when the Dul Hasti project was established in the Kishtwar town local population of Kishtwar town has changed their traditional employment and engaged in other occupation for earning their better livelihood.

EMPLOYMENT OPPORTUNITY

In district Kishtwar it is analysed through the present study that with the start of construction of the project, the local unemployed youth got an opportunity to work with the contractors as per their qualification and experience. They got skilled and unskilled jobs, which helped in earning their livelihood and in due course they also gained the technical knowledge. The local employment opportunity also helped in raising the standard of living of the local population. For infrastructural development of the project, such as colonies, roads and related works NHPC has engaged contractors as a result of which the local people who are in this field have been benefitted a lot. Due to Dul Hasti project in Kishtwar many local people have been employed in project. It has been found that before the Dul Hasti project people of Kishtwar were engaged in agricultural activities and small business, it is also seen that previously their socio- economic condition was not well.

SUGGESTIONS

Some of the suggestions regarding the consequences of development are as follows

- The state has to ensure that benefits of development are shared in a proportionate manner giving due consideration to the well-being of the affected families.
- The affected people should be the equal partners in the decision making regarding the project. They have to be treated as co-partners in the process of development so that they become partners rather than victims of development.
- The affected people should be given first preference for the employment in the projects. Their prime requirements of getting

employment, making them accessible to irrigation water and investing in local infrastructures of the region, e.g. School, Colleges etc. are some of the expectation of the public from the hydro power project authorities should be taken into consideration.

- There should be proper rehabilitation and resettlement policies framed by the government so that everyone can take the benefit of development.

REFERENCES

Baboo, Balagovind. (1922). "Big Dams and Tribal: the Case study of the Hirakund Dam oustess in Orissa", *Social Action*, 41 (3). 288-303.

Baviskar, Amita. (1997). "Ecology and Development in India: A Field and its Future", *Sociological Bulletin*, 46 (2). 193-207.

Cernea, M. M. (1990). *Poverty Risks from population displacement in water resources development*, HIID Development Discussion paper No. 355, Harvard University: Cambridge.

Cernea, Michael. (2000). *Risks and Reconstruction: Experiences of Resettlers and Refugees*, New York: Oxford Publishers.

Dube, S. C. (1998). *Modernization and Development*. New Delhi: Vistaar Publishers.

Dhawan, B. D. (1990). *The Big Dams:Claims and counter Claims Commonwealth*. New Delhi: Sage Publications.

Fernandes, W. (1991). "Power and Powerlessness: Development Projects and Displacements of tribal", *Social Action*, 41 (3): 243-270.

Gajananda, K. (2011). *Dam or No Dam*. Imphal: Sangai Express, www.thesangaiexpress.com).

Guha, Ramachandra. (1989). *The unquiet woods: Ecological change and peasant Resistance in the Himalaya*. New Delhi: Oxford University press.

Kothari, Smitu. (1995). "Development Displacement", *Sociological Bulletin*, 11(5): 45-56.

McCully, Patrick. (1998). *The ecology and Politics of Large dams*. Delhi: Orient Longman Publishers.

Menezes. (1991). "Compensation for Project and Displacement", *Economic and Political weekly*, 26(3). 24-32.

Robert. K. Merton. (1968). *Social Theory and Social Structure*. Oxford University Press.

Mishra, O. P. (2001). *Forced Migration in the South Asian Region*: Kolkata, University of Jadavpur.

Murickan, Jose. (2003). *Development induced Displacement: Case of Kerala*, Jaipur: Rawat Publication.

Parasuraman, S. (1999). "The Development dilemma: Displacement in India", *The Hague*: Macmillan Institute of Social Studies.

Patnaik, S. M. (1996). "Tribe and Displacement: Social implication of Rehabilitation", *Journal of Human Ecology*, 11(4): 299-314.

Saksena, H. S, and Sen. C. (1998). *Putting people last: A Study of Displacement and rehabilitation in Sonebhadra, U.P*, New Delhi: Inter India Publishers.

Udombana, N. J. (2000). "The Third World and the Right to Development: Agenda for the Third Millennium", *Human Rights Quarterly*, 22(2): 22-24.

World Commission on Dams, (WCD). (1999). "Displacement, resettlement, rehabilitation, reparation and development", *Thematic review, scoping paper*, Capetown: WCD, 1999.

CHAPTER- XIII
SCIENCE EDUCATION AMONG KASHMIRI FEMALES

A STUDY OF DISTRICT ANANTNAG

GOUSIA YASIN

Introduction

Every subject finds a place in curriculum only on the basis of its values. Science gained importance and has become a compulsory subject at secondary stage only due to its multifarious values. Science is taught for variety of reasons. It promotes creativity, inventions and discoveries. Science is a process by which we increase and refine understanding about ourselves and of the universe through continuous observation, experimentation and verification. Science is organized common sense, is search for truth is a process that unveils the mystery of nature.

Science Education among Kashmiri Females

Scientific temper means a value frame, an outlook for the world and approach to ones world of deeds and actions. Scientific temper is a value as well as a method of attaining human rights under humanism as the only value worth striving for in the trouble torn social formations from domestic to international levels. In our culturally plural society education should faster universal and eternal values; oriented towards the unity and integration of our people such education should eliminate obscurantism, religious fanaticism, violence, superstition and fatalism. It was found that in the earlier times science education was less among Kashmiri females. The reasons for this were effect of traditionalism, conservative nature of parents, poor economic conditions. The investigator found that these things are now a days less among the people especially among Kashmiri females. Now traditionalism has its least effect on our Kashmiri society. Parents are sending their daughters to achieve higher and higher education particularly science education. Now females are participating in every competitive exam. Science education has increased the abilities and talents of Kashmiri females.

Science Education and Social Change

According to Huxley, "Science is an organized common sense. It is that syntactical knowledge which is arrived at through observations, experiments, yielding observation based knowledge which leads to the genesis of theory and laws which culminate into fruit full inventions and discoveries". The term science is a cumulative term; it refers to and includes within its ambit all developments which take place in all fields governing human life. Primarily science refers to technological developments and sub-servant developments their too. Upon further ramifying, science includes philosophical, educational, sociological, cultural behavior and other developments which govern the human conduct. From recent few decades there has been tremendous scientific modernization which has landed human mind into a sea of surprise and perplexion. We had never foreseen that what we witness today. Science has traversed the frontiers of all spheres of knowledge and has unveiled mysteries of nature. Be it information technology, be it space exploration, be it medical science, be it physical science or any other special branch of science, it has remarkably conquered all hidden treasures of nature and has lost nothing of itself.

Research investigator found that 72.85% respondents were from rural and 27.14% were from urban. It is so because the research was carried in rural areas particularly.

Table 1.2

S. No.	Marital Status	Number	Percentage
1	Single	68	97.14%
2	Married	02	02.85%
	Total	70	100%

Out of 70 respondents 97% were single and only 02.85% were married. It is so because the investigator collected the data from educational institutes (students).

Table 1.3

S. No.	Type of family	Number	Percentage
1	Nuclear	59	84.02%
2	Joint	11	15.71%
	Total	70	100%

Issues and Problems in the Sociology of Jammu & Kashmir

Out of 70 respondents 84% were from nuclear from nuclear families and 15.71% belonged to joint families. It is because of improvements/ technology/ social change that societies have changed from joint to nuclear families.

Table 1.4

S. No.	Occupation	Number	Percentage
1	Agriculture	08	11.42%
2	Govt. Employee	45	64.28%
3	Private Employee	06	08.57%
4	Other	11	15.71%
	Total	70	100%

Out of 70 respondents family occupation of 11.42% is agriculture, 64.28% is govt. employee, 08.57% private employee and 15.71% is other.

Table 1.5

S. No.	Family income	Number	Percentage
1	-5000	11	15.71%
2	5000-20000	44	62.85%
3	20,000-50,000	13	18.57%
4	+50,000	02	02.85%
	Total	70	100%

This table shows that a very good number of respondents belong to the average family income group.

Table 1.6

S. No.	Family attitude	Number	Percentage
1	Encouraging	60	85.71%
2	Discouraging	10	14.28%
	Total	70	100%

Issues and Problems in the Sociology of Jammu & Kashmir

Out of 70 respondents the research investigator found that the family attitude to science education is 85.71% encouraging and 14.28% discouraging.

Table 1.7

S. No.	Professional risk	Number	Percentage
1	Yes	27	38.57%
2	No	43	61.42%
	Total	70	100%

This table shows that there is awareness among parents towards science education of females. They are allowing their daughters to go for it.

Table 1.8

S. No.	Science education in contemporary times	Number	Percentage
1	Development of society	39	55.71%
2	Development of self	12	17.14%
3	Better opportunities	11	15.71%
4	Other	08	11.41%
	Total	70	100%

55.71% respondents said that science education is for development of society, 17.14%% said for development of self, 15.71% said for better opportunities and 11.411% said other.

Table 1.9

S. No.	Traditionalism on science education	Number	Percentage
1	Yes	34	48.57%
2	No	36	51.42%
	Total	70	100%

Investigator found that 48.57% respondents are in favor of effect of rationalism of science education and 51.42% respondents were not.

Table 1.10

S. No.	Economic condition	Number	Percentage
1	Yes	67	95. 72%

Issues and Problems in the Sociology of Jammu & Kashmir

2	No	3	4.28%
	Total	70	100%

Almost 95.72% respondents said that economic conditions are responsible for taking or leaving science education. Science education is costly so it is greatly connected with economy.

Table 1.11

S. No.	Schemes/ Scholarships	Number	Percentage
1	Yes	20	28.58
2	No	50	71.42
	Yes	70	100%

The field investigator found that there is lack of awareness about scholarships provided in science education. The authority system is even fraud. They are not doing justice with the students.

Table 1.12

S. No.	Job opportunity	Number	Percentage
1	Yes	46	65.72%
2	No	24	34.28%
	Total	70	100%

Major portion of respondent said that there more job opportunity in science field as compared to other fields. This table shows that more no. of students can be adjusted in the jobs which the science education provides them.

Table 1.13

S. No.	Science education helps you in terms of	Number	Percentage
1	Perform better	23	32.85%
2	Aware surroundings	20	28.57%
3	Edge over others	0	
4	Cause and effect relationship	21	30%
	Any other		

Issues and Problems in the Sociology of Jammu & Kashmir

5	Total	06	08.58%
		70	100%

Investigator found that 32.85% respondents said that science education helps you in terms of performing better.

Table 1.14

S. No.	Science education has made women change	Number	Percentage
1	Change	67	95.71%
2	No change	0	
3	Both	02	02.85%
4	None	1	01.42%
	Total	70	100%

Investigator found that 95.71% respondents said that science education has made women change. It is because science education has made women aware about each and every thing related to their life. The women understood the cause and effect relationship of every phenomenon. So it leads change in humans and particularly in women.

Table 1.15

S. No.	Science education and betterment of society	Number	Percentage
1	Better living standard	15	21.42%
2	Better opportunity	5	07.14%
3	Overall development	45	64.28%
4	Any other	5	07.15%
	Total	70	100%

Investigator found that 64.28% respondents said that science education leads to overall development of society. 21.42% said that it leads to better living standard. 07.14% said it gives better opportunities. In short science education leads to the betterment of society in terms of all these.

Issues and Problems in the Sociology of Jammu & Kashmir

Table 1.16

S. No.	Science education and status of women	Number	Percentage
1	Raised	66	94.28%
2	Declined	1	01.42%
3	No impact	2	02.85%
4	Any other	1	01.42%
	Total	70	100%

Out of 70 respondents 94.28% said that it has raised the status of women.

Table 1.17

S. No.	Religion restricts women	Number	Percentage
1	Yes	20	28.57%
2	No	50	71.43%
	Total	70	100%

Investigator came to know that religion has fewer roles in taking or leaving science education.

Table 1.18

S. No.	Reorientation	Number	Percentage
1	Yes	70	100%
2	No		
	Total	70	100%

100% respondents are in favor that science education needs to be reoriented.

Table 1.19

S. No.	Role of mass media	Number	Percentage
1	Acts as barriers	1	01.42%

Issues and Problems in the Sociology of Jammu & Kashmir

2	Acts as promoters	66	94.28%
3	No effect	3	04.28%
4	Any other		
	Total	70	100%

Investigator found that mass media plays a great role in spreading science education.

Table 1.20

S. No.	Promotional programmes through	Number	Percentage
1	T.V	5	07.15%
2	Radio	4	05.71%
3	News paper	3	04.28%
4	Posters	0	
5	All above	58	82.85%
	Total	70	100%

Investigator found that promotional programmes should b encouraged through all above because some like T.V., some are listening radio etc.

Suggestions

1. Govt. should establish more science colleges, medical colleges and universities. It needs to be reoriented even at the primary level which is the base of all education.
2. Co-education acts as a hindrance in taking science education among Kashmiri females. Govt. should open separate colleges for girls.
3. There should be reservation for girls at the university level also.
4. Govt. should organize more seminars, debates to aware the people about science education.

References

1. Ahuja Ram, Research Methods, Rawat Publications Published in 2001.
2. Devi Laxmi, encyclopedia of Social Change, Anmol Publication New Delhi 110002 Published in year 1996.
3. Dutt Suresh, Women and Education, ANMOL Publications New Delhi, 110002 Published in 1992.
4. Koul Lokesh, Methodology of Educational Research, Vikas Publishing House, New Delhi Published in 1989.
5. Professor N.A. Nadeem, journal of Applied Research in Education published in 2008

CHAPTER- XIV
THE HISTORY OF CULTURE AND TRADITION

KASHMIRI PANDITS IN JAMMU AND KASHMIR

UMAR MANZOOR MIR

Introduction

Like its scenic beauty, Kashmir valley is even famous for its cultural heritage. The valley of Kashmir is very rich as far as different aspects of its culture are concerned. Right through ages, it has adopted and assimilated components of various civilizations and religions. The amalgamation of Hindu, Muslim and Buddhist Philosophies has added colour and fragrance to the Kashmiri culture resulting into a composite culture based on humanism, secularism and tolerance. Besides, it has borrowed certain features from its adjacent regions like Central Asia also. To sum up, the valley of Kashmir has a unique and peculiar culture, which is reflected in different walks of life. Some aspects of Kashmiri culture are given below:

Belief System

To understand the cultural basis of a particular community, the study of its religious beliefs is very important. Religion forms an all-pervasive component of the culture of a community. Kashmir is inhabited by believers of Islam, Hinduism and Sikhism. A few Christians and Buddhists also live there. Islam is the dominant religion in Kashmir Valley. There are different opinions regarding the spread of Islam in the valley. Some historians are of the view that a Syrian by the name of Hamim bin Sam was the first Muslim to settle in Kashmir. He came to Kashmir with Raja Dahir's son Jasiya, after the latter fled to Delhi when Muhammed Bin Qasim defeated Dahir.

The conversion of Gyalpo Rinchana, the ruler of Kashmir to Islam at the hands of Abdul Rahman Bulbul, facilitated conversion of a large number of people to Islam. However, the mass conversion of the majority of population took place after the propagation of the new faith by Hazrat Mir Syed Ali Hamadani and his associates. Mir Syed Ali Hamadani, popularly known as Shah-I-Hamadan (in Kashmir), visited the valley three times and brought with him seven hundred disciples, known as Sadaat, from Central Asia. These Sadaat visited different parts of Kashmir and engaged them in the propagation of Islam. The present dominant position of Islam in Kashmir can be attributed partially to the efforts of these saints and the forced conversions into Islam as by some of the Muslim rulers of Kashmir.

Hinduism forms the second major religion of Kashmir. It is the oldest religion of the valley. Its followers are scattered throughout the valley and their presence is felt in every sphere of life. The community is highly educated. They belong to the upper stratum of the society and are generally known as Pandits i.e. the learned men. Kashmiri Pandits have been profoundly religious people. Religion has played a pivotal role in shaping their customs, rituals, rites, festivals, fasts, ceremonies, food habits etc. Kashmir is widely known as the birth-place of 'Kashmir Shaivism' – a philosophy expounding the unity of Shiva and Shakti. Hence, Shaiva bhakti and Tantra constitute the substratum of the ritualistic worship of Kashmiri Pandits on which the tall edifice of the worship of Vishnu (Krishna and Ram), Lakshmi and Saraswati, and a host of other deities has been built.

Sikhism forms the third major religion of Kashmir valley. However, in comparison to Muslims and Hindus, Sikhs are fewer in number. Opinions vary as to how they established themselves in Kashmir. Some people are of the view that "they came into Kashmir with the lieutenants of Ranjit Singh, but some state that there were Punjabi Brahmins already living in Kashmir and they embraced Sikhism when the valley passed into the hands of Ranjit Singh." (Walter Lawrence : The valley of Kashmir). Another opinion holds that they came to Kashmir during the time of Pathans in the service of Raja Sukhjewan, a Hindu of Shikarpur, who was sent as Governor of Kashmir by Timur Shah of Kabul, in about 1775 A.D. It is also said that "the advent of the Sikh faith in Kashmir begins with the visit of Guru Nanak Devji (1460-1539) to the valley in 1517."

Kashmir has been a great centre of learning for several centuries. It has been a major centre of Buddhist learning for nearly a millennium during which period a sizeable number of revered Kashmiri Buddhist scholars traveled as far as Sri Lanka in the South and Tibet and China in the North. The contribution of these scholars commands a place of pride in the extant Buddhist philosophy. Unfortunately, this tradition was brought to an almost abrupt end by the Pathan and Mongol invaders in the 14th century. Though the advent of Islam produced a clash of civilizations, it also brought into being a 'composite culture' in which saintly figures (Reshi, Pir, Mot, Shah) came to be revered and respected equally by the polytheistic Hindu as well as the monotheistic Muslim.

Birth, Marriage and Death

The customs related to birth, marriage and death among Hindu and Muslim communities of Kashmir are very elaborate. Although there exist some differences in the rites performed by these communities, most of the customs run similar. A brief attempt has been made to trace the customs of these two communities.

Birth

The birth ceremony of a Hindu is an elaborate one, with mystic figures chalked on the floor, fire, pots and pestle being worshipped. The exact time and date of birth is carefully noted by the family astrologer. On the fourth day of the child's birth, a special feast composed of sesame, walnuts and sugar fried in oil, is prepared and sent to relatives and friends. It is called teil Panjiri. On the same day mother's parents send some special food to their daughters house. On the 7th day, the ceremony of bathing the mother and the child (Sundar Sran) is performed and on this same day the naming ceremony takes place. On the eleventh day, the house is swept and the bed is remade. The family Brahmin is called and a ceremony called kah Neathar is performed in which the mother takes five products of the cow, namely, milk, butter, ghee, dung and urine, thus purifying herself. A hawan is also performed on this day. Special vegetarian/ no vegetarian dishes are prepared on the occasion. Pieces of paper (burzI) are burnt in an earthen plate to ward off evil. Seven plates of special food are served to the paternal aunts of the baby. This is exclusively a women's ceremony. On this day the mother's parents send 'trIy phot' (wife's basket) which contains clothes, rotis, sugar, spices, cash for the newborn, and its parents and grandparents. The astrologers cast the child's horoscope (Zatuk). When the child is of one month, the ceremony called masInethIr is observed. The ears of the child are pierced in its sixth month. On this day food is distributed among relatives and friends. In the third year, the ceremony known as Zara Kasa is performed. When the male child attains seven years of age, the thread ceremony called Mekhal or Yagnopavit is observed and from then the child is considered a true Brahmin. This is considered the beginning of Brahmachari life, the first stage of Hindu life where knowledge and wisdom are attained. After this, the Guru (family-purohit) whispers the Gayatri Mantra and the child is directed to recite this mantra every morning after bath. The family priest invokes the protection of sixty four deities. The boy stands on a mystic figure drawn on the ground while the women sing around him and coins are shed over this head. He is then taken to the riverbank where he performs his first prayer ceremony (Sandhya).

Marriage

Hindu marriage is not a social contract, but rather it is a religious institution, a sacrament or a spiritual or divine element which binds the permanent relationship between the husband and wife. The husband and wife are not only responsible for each other, but they also owe allegiance to the divine element. This mystic aspect of Hindu marriage necessitates a number of symbols. The marriage creates a new bond between the bride and the groom. They have to rear up this union by dedicating their entire energy in the direction of their common interest and ideal.

Issues and Problems in the Sociology of Jammu & Kashmir

Traditionally, amongst Hindus, marriage was possible only between the families which have had no kinship for seven generations on the paternal side and four generations on the maternal side. Once the boy and the girl consent to join as man and wife, i.e., if they consent for marriage, the parents of both the girl and boy will meet in a temple in the company of the middleman (if there is any). In some families, a family member is selected from both the sides to vow that they would join the two families in a new bond of kinship. This ritual is known as Kasam-drIy. This is followed by a formal engagement ceremony (taakh or gandun) in which some members of the groom's family and relatives visit the bride's place to partake in a rich feast. The party brings cloths, preferably a Saree and some ornaments, which the bride is made to wear by her would be sister–in-law. During this ceremony, the two parties exchange flowers and vow to join together through wedlock. A younger brother or sister of the bride accompanies the groom's party with a gift of clothes for the groom. After this function, the two families begin to make preparations for the marriage ceremony which is held on some auspicious day after consulting a purohit.

Several rituals are associated with marriage whose observance begins nearly a week before the wedding day. Such ritual is known as GarInavai (literally get madeup) in this the hair of the bride is let loose. This is followed by malI məənZ or saatI məənz (first henna or auspicious henna) when henna is applied to the bride and the groom by their respective mothers and aunts. Close relatives and neighbors' attend these rituals. Meenzyraath (henna night) is the first major event when all the relatives-men, women and children in the extended families-assemble at the girl's and the boy's respective places. This is a night of rejoicing and feasting. The evening meal is followed by a series of ceremonial acts. Henna is pasted on the hands and feet of the bride and the groom and almost every young boys, women and girls apply henna on their hands when elderly women sing traditional songs. Before applying henna, maternal aunt (maami) washes the feet and hands of the bride and the groom while the paternal aunt (bua) applies henna. The maternal aunt (maasi) burns incense to ward off evil. Meanwhile women, girls and boys sing traditional ditties as well as popular songs appropriate to the occasion.

While the singing & henna pasting is on, the bride as well as the groom is given a thorough bath (kani shraan) by aunts and sisters –in–law to prepare them for Devgun, the entrance of Devtas. After the ceremonial bath, the boy and the girl wear clothes brought by their respective maternal uncles. The bride is made to wear dejhuur-'a gold ornament', and kalpush-'a variety of headgear'.

Dejhuur is tied to a gold chain, which is provided by the groom's family on the wedding day to complete the holy alliance between Shiva – the groom, and Parvati -the bride.

Issues and Problems in the Sociology of Jammu & Kashmir

Devgun is the religious ritual performed after the bath. The family purohit performs a small yajna on this occasion. 'Devgun', it is believed, transforms the bride and the groom into 'Devtas'.

On the wedding day the groom wears a colorful dress with saffron – colored turban on his head. He is made to stand on a beautifully made Rangoli (vyug) in the compound of the house, where parents, relatives and friends put garlands made of fresh plucked flowers, of cardamom and currency notes round the groom's neck. A cousin holds a flower-decked umbrella to protect the groom against evil. Conch-shells are blown, ditties are sung and the groom's party moves towards the bride's place usually in cars and other modes of transport.

Conch-shells announce the arrival of the groom and his party at the bride's place where the lane leading to the main entrance of the house is beautifully decorated with colorful flowers and dyed saw-dust. Upon entering the compound of the bride's house, the groom is welcomed by traditional songs sung by the bride's relations. He is put on a rangoli where the bride draped in a colourful Silk Saree is made to stand beside him on his left side. There is another round of garlanding from the girl's relatives. Then the mother of the bride comes with a thali of small lighted lamps made of kneaded rice flour and an assortment of sweets and makes the groom and the bride eat from the same piece of sweet, a couple of times. After this the bride is taken back into the house and the groom is made to stand at the main door of the house for a short dvaar puja, 'door–prayer'. The groom's party joins the bride's relatives in a rich feast. Meanwhile the bride and the groom are seated in a beautifully decorated room for a series of rituals and ceremonies amidst chanting of Sanskrit mantras for several hours with little breaks in between. During these ceremonies, the bride is supported by her maternal uncle. The purohits of the two families recite mantras and make the bride, groom and their parents perform a number of rituals with fire (agni) as the witness. The boy and the girl vow to live together in prosperity and adversity, in joy as well as in sorrow until death separates them. Lagan, as this ceremony is called, is followed by posh puja 'showering of flowers' in which a red shawl, held at four edges by four people, is spread over the bride and the groom and amidst recitation of shlokas all the elderly people shower flowers on the two 'devtas'. After this ceremony, the bride and the groom are taken to the kitchen and made to eat from the same plate.

A is drawn on the floor of the compound and the bride and the groom are made to stand on it. Now the bride joins the groom to the groom's place where yet another rangoli is drawn and the bride and the groom are again made to stand on it. Here the groom's party relaxes and the bride is made to wear 'aTh', the gold chain that is attached to dejhuur. Her hair and head-gear (tarangI) are tied and she is made to wear a saree given to her by the groom's family.

Issues and Problems in the Sociology of Jammu & Kashmir

After this, they return to the bride's place with a small party comprising groom's father, brothers, sisters, brothers-in-law, and a couple of friends. She is now a guest at her parent's place. The groom's party asks the bride's parents to send her (the bride) to her family (the in-laws). After a small tea party, the party leaves for the groom's place. A younger brother/ sister/ cousin of the bride accompany the party to the groom's place. On the next day, depending upon the mahuurat (auspicious day), the newly married couple visits the wife's parents. This visit is known as 'satraath or 'phirI saal. Upon reaching the wife's parent's place, the man and wife are welcomed with aalath – a thali with water, rice, coins and flowers.

The nuptials in their utterances, promises, and hopes symbolize a great social transition in the life of the bride and the bridegroom. They have to earn their own livelihood, procreate children and discharge their obligations towards Gods, parents, children and other creatures of the world. The nuptial ceremonies address all aspects of married life: biological, physical, and mental.

During the first year of marriage, the girl's parents send gifts to the groom in the form of cash, clothes, sweets, fruits, & cooked food. This is being sent on a number of occasions like birthday (prasad in the form of walnuts and baked bread etc.) Shivratri (herits boog), Janamashtami and Diwali (fruits, sweets etc), KhetsI maavas (pulaav etc.) etc. During the month of Magar, a special ceremony known as shishur is solemnized. On this occasion the bride is provided with a special kangri-'a brazier used during winter', and shishur 'til seeds wrapped in a piece of silk'. On this day, close relatives, especially ladies are invited and the girl's parents send gifts to their daughter in the form of clothes or cash.

The marriage ceremony of a Muslim has great resemblance to that of a Hindu. Even here the services of a match-maker are availed to get a suitable bride. After the match is fixed, the betrothal ceremony, known as Nishan, takes place in which the groom's father, with some relatives, visits and takes presents to the girl's house. The visit is later paid back by the bride's father and her relatives. Later a date is fixed for the marriage, which is duly solemnized in the Nikah ceremony in which the priest delivers a sermon highlighting the purpose behind the marriage. In the same ceremony a formal consent is elicited from the groom and the bride and the amount of Mehr (dowry) to be paid by the groom to the bride is fixed. On the preceding day of marriage, the groom's father sends some mehndi to the bride's house with which she stains her feet and hands, while the women folk sing traditional folk songs. This night of celebrations and dying the hands and feet is known as Menzhat (The night of applying mehndi). Next day, the groom visits the bride's house alongwith his friends and relatives (Baratis) and a feast is served to the guests. After the feast is over, the Rukhsati or departure of the bride to her father-in-law's house takes place.

A female relative known as dudh moj accompanies the bride who gives her instructions regarding the formalities to be observed. On reaching her father-in-law's house, the bride is taken to a room which is specially decorated for her. After the bride's arrival, her mother-in-law takes the veil off the bride's face and, at the same time, the bride passes on a handkerchief containing some golden ornament or cash to her and this is regarded as the mother-in-law's perquisite or hash-kant. A great feast is served on this day in the groom's house in which the world famous and choicest wazwan dishes are served.

Death

When a person breathes his / her last, his/her mortal remains are washed in water. and cotton buds are put into his / her ears and nostrils. A coin is placed at its lips. The whole body is covered in a white shroud and tied with a thread (neeryvan). The body is then placed on a plank of wood and four persons take the coffin on their shoulders to the cremation ground. The eldest son of the deceased carries an earthen pitcher in his hand and leads the coffin. The coffin is placed on the ground near the cremation ground, and the family members, relatives and friends are allowed to have a last glimpse of the deceased's face. The coffin is then taken to the cremation ground and put on a pyre. It is the duty of the eldest son to light the pyre. From the second day of one's death, for about eight days, the eldest son or daughter of the departed one, call upon their departed father/mother a couple of times.

On the fourth day of cremation, the sons, relatives and family friends go to the cremation ground to gather ashes (EsrakI). It is immersed into a nearby river / stream and a part of it is put in an earthen pitcher and taken to Haridwar for immersion in the holy Ganges.

On the 10th day, the sons of the deceased along with relatives and the family purohit go to a river bank where sons' heads are shaved and a Shraadha is performed. On the 11th day, the sons and daughters perform an elaborate shraadha under the guidance of a purohit. The ceremony ends with aahuuti given to agni invoking almost all the deities, major rivers, temple towns, mountains, and lakes of South Asia. On this day the daughters too pay dakshina to the purohit and arrange food for the families of their brothers. Favorite vegetarian food is prepared in the name of the deceased. Burning of oil lamps on this day is meant to provide light to the deceased in the 'other' world.

For the first three months, a shraadha is performed for every fifteen days i.e. on the 30th , 45th, 60th , 75th and 90th day of death. An elaborate shraadha is held on the 180th day (Shadmoos), 6th month. The shraadha on the first death anniversary (veharveed) too is an elaborate one. On this day the close kins of the deceased one assemble to perform both shadmoos and

Issues and Problems in the Sociology of Jammu & Kashmir

vəharvəəD. After this, a shraadha is performed every year on the death anniversary.

Muslims believe in the life after death. When a Muslim approaches his death, he is laid on bed with his head towards the north or east. After death, the corpse is bathed and wrapped in white cloth (Kafan). The body is then carried in a coffin (Tabut) to the graveyard where it is buried in the grave. At the time of burial, quranic verses are recited by the side of the grave and supplications and prayers are made for the departed soul. There is active mourning in the family of the dead for three days and on the fourth day chaharum is observed.

Dress Pattern

As far as the dress of early inhabitants of Kashmir is concerned, there exists literary as well as archaeological evidence. According to this evidence "the costume of the male population consisted of a lower garment (adhararan sukha), an upper garment (angaraksaka) and turban (sirahasta." (S.R. Bakhshi, 1996, Kashmir Through Ages).

There is little difference in the dress worn by Muslims and Hindus. Both Muslims and Hindus are seen wearing the local kurtan' ye:za:rI or pə:Ia:mI shalwar-kameez. The ordinary headdress of a common Kashmiri is a cotton skullcap. Muslim women wear Phirak-yezar (lady suit) while as Hindu women opt for Sari.

The nature of the dress varies according to the season. In the winters, they wear garments made of wool, while as in summer cotton garments are used. The low temperature of the winter compels people to employ woolen Pherans (Kashmiri gowns), which spreads from the neck and extends to cover knees. It helps to "exclude the air and to keep in the heat of the Kangar when a man sits down on the ground".

Kangri forms an indispensable part of Kashmiri culture. It is "a small earthenware bowl of a quaint shape, held in a frame of wicker-work." (Lawrence, The Valley of Kashmir). With hot embers in it, it is used under Pheran to keep a person warm during freezing cold winters. Besides the Pheran, woolen blankets and shawls are also frequently used during the winters.

In their make-up and nature, Kashmiri garments are unique and unparalleled. However, it needs to be said that due to the cultural impact of the west, Kashmiri youth are now adopting the western dress at a very rapid rate. Also the well-to-do and the government employees are at ease wearing the western suits so much so that pants, coats, jackets and T-shirts are no longer seen as alien to the Kashmiri culture.

Jewellery

The women of Kashmir, like any other woman, do not lag behind in their fondness for ornaments. The various kinds of ornaments worn by them include anklets, bracelets, earrings, necklaces etc. These ornaments are generally made of gold and silver but "sometimes beautiful colours of flowers and leaves and fruits are designed by studding jewellery with precious and semi-precious stones, shades such as jade, agate, turquise, rubies and the gold stone. There are necklaces made in yellow base metal, set with imitation emeralds and sapphires." The Kashmiri ornaments are unique in their designs and "are unlike those of other places, that is, kaleidoscopic arrangement of geometric figures. On the other hand they carry the forms of products like almond, grapes, cherries and birds like myna, sparrow and bulbul. On these ornaments are not engraved horrifying figures of snakes, dragons and wild animals." In Sufi's words, "The Kashmiri jewellers seem to have had nature as their model in most ornaments."

Central Asia has influenced the jewellery making of Kashmir valley to a greater extent. The influence of Mughals can also be easily traced.

The ornaments worn by Hindus and Muslims are, to a great extent, alike. These include the ornaments of head, ear, neck and wrists. The ornaments of the head include jiggni and tikka, which are worn on the forehead. They are generally triangular, semi-circular and circular in shape and are made of gold and silver and are fringed with hanging pearls and gold leaves.

The ornaments of the ear include Bala, Deji-hor, Atahor, Kanadoor, Jumaka, Deji-hor and Kana-Vaji. Deji-hor is an indispensable ornament for Kashmiri Hindu married women, as it symbolizes Hindu wedlock. Halqa-band, Kanthi, Sagalar, necklace, tulsi, raz are ornaments for the neck.

The ornaments for wrists include bangar, gunus, dula, kor etc. They are made of solid gold and silver.

Food and Drink

Mere cultural survey of a nation cannot be confined to the study of religion, literature and art of a particular place. It includes a gamut of other things like food and drink, dress and ornaments etc. Food system of a community forms one of the important aspects of culture of that community.

Kashmiris are gross eaters. Majority of the Muslims of the valley arc non-vegetarians even Hindus are very rare vegetarian.

Rice and knolkhol (haakh-batI) are the traditional stable diet of Kashmiris. The use of a wide variety of spices, e.g., aniseed powder, turmeric powder, chilly powder, ginger powder, black-pepper, cardamom, saffron etc., is very common among Kashmiris. Besides knolkhol they relish beans, potato, spinach, lotus-stalk, sonchal, raddish, turnip, cabbage, cauliflower, wild mushroom cheese, and an assortment of local greens like liisI, vopal haakh, nunar, vosti haakh, hand. However, the main specaility of Kashmiri cuisiue

Issues and Problems in the Sociology of Jammu & Kashmir

is non-vegetarian food. The major non-vegetarian preparations of the KP include kəliyi, roganjosh, matsh, kabar gah, yakhIny, tabakh naaTI, tsok tsarwan etc.

Rice serves as the main staple food for Kashmiris. The chief staple food of the valley include rice and other grains cooked as porridge, or ground into flour and made into bread, vegetables, oil, salt and pepper. The boiled rice is taken with vegetables or mutton. Being found in abundance, poultry (fowls, ducks and geese) is frequently used. Fish is also heir favorite food.

Kashmiris are very fond of tea, which may be either salty or sweet. Salt tea is commonly found here but Kahwa (sweet tea) of Kashmir is known for its taste. Kashmir is very famous for its fruits. The apple, pear, plum, peach, apricot is the principal fruit products of the valley. Kashmiri dry fruits like almonds, walnuts etc., are famous world over. Among the spices used pepper, black-pepper, ginger etc may be mentioned.

REFERENCES

Bakshi, S.R. (1997). Kashmir: History & People. Sarup & Sons. p. 103. Retrieved 8 July 2012.

Barbara Anne Brower, Barbara Rose Johnston. Disappearing Peoples? Indigenous groups and ethnic minorities in South & Central Asia. Left Coast Press, Indiana University. p. 138. Retrieved 29 Dec 2012.

Bose, Sumantra (2005). Kashmir: roots of conflict, paths to peace. Harvard University Press.

Dhar, Triloki Nath. Kashmiri Pandit Community: A Profile. Mittal Publications, Darya Ganj, New Delhi. p. 73.

Essa, Assad (2 August 2011). "Kashmiri Pandits: Why we never fled Kashmir". aljazeera.com. Retrieved 15 August 2012.

Bamzai, Prithivi Nath Kaul (1994). Culture and political history of Kashmir, Volume 1. M.D. Publications Pvt. Ltd. pp. 191–192

Kaw, M. K. (2004). Kashmir and it's people: studies in the evolution of Kashmiri society. Volume 4 of KECSS research series: Culture and heritage of Kashmir. APH Publishing. p. 90.

Lawrence Walter, (1895) The Valley of Kashmir, London H. Frowde.

Madan, T. N. (2008), "Kashmir, Kashmiris, Kashmiriyat: An Introductory Essay", in Rao, Aparna, The Valley of Kashmir: The Making and Unmaking of a Composite Culture?, Delhi: Manohar.

Metcalf, Barbara; Metcalf, Thomas R. (2006), A Concise History of Modern India (Cambridge Concise Histories), Cambridge and New York: Cambridge University Press. Pp. 372.

Pandita, K, Rahul (2013). Our Moon has Blood Clots: The Exodus of the Kashmiri Pandits. Vintage Books / Random House. p. 255.

Rajbali Pandey Hindu Saṁskāras: Socio-religious Study of the Hindu Sacraments.

Rai, Mridu (2004), Hindu Rulers, Muslim Subjects: Islam, Rights, and the History of Kashmir, Princeton University Press/Permanent Black. Pp. xii, 335.

Stein, Mark Aurel (1989) [1900]. Kalhana's Rajatarangini: a chronicle of the kings of Kasmir, Volume 1 (Reprinted ed.). Motilal Banarsidass. pp. 106–108. Retrieved 18 July 2011.

Toshakhani, Sasisekhara. Rites and rituals of Kashmiri Brahmins. New Delhi: Pentagon Press, 2010.

Zutshi, Chitraleka (2008). "Shrines, Political Authority, and Religious Identities in Late-Nineteenth and Early-Twentieth-century Kashmir". In Rao, Aparna. The Valley of Kashmir: The Making and Unmaking of a Composite Culture?. Delhi: Manohar. pp. 235–258.

Webliography

http://ikashmir.net/festivals/festivals2.html

http://ikashmir.net/festivals/index.html
http://ikashmir.net/festivals/festivals2.html
http://koausa.org/music/festivals/index.html
Kashmir Hindu Foundation (KHF)
Kashmir-information.com
Panun Kashmir: A Homeland for Kashmiri Pandits

SUMMARY

It can be generalized that Pakhtoon woman play very little part in their social life. They spend most of time in household activities and having less contribution in outdoor activities. It is an observed fact that Pakhtoons sustain their patterns of norms and values as the most valuable property in the course of life. These values have developed the unique concept of shame and honor, which is inevitably necessary to keep an approved mode of status and role in the Pakhtoon social order. Gender patterns are followed strictly with no choice of getting out of them. The women role and status is determined in Pakhtoon society by the male.

There is no denying the fact that both girls and boys engage in the worst forms of child labour. However, it is important to realize that due to certain societal expectations, duties and responsibilities placed on girls, they are often more vulnerable to exploitation. It is essential to understand the culture and environment in which child labour occurs in order to address all of the root causes of child labour, including gender bias. Gender discrimination often results in disparity in girls' enrolment, high dropout rate and their early involvement in economic activities.

The OBCs are entitled to 27 per cent reservations in public sector employment and higher education. In the constitution, OBCs are described as "socially and educationally backward classes", and government is enjoined to ensure their social and educational development. Mandal Commission report of 1980 quoted OBC population at 52 per cent and recommended 27 percent reservation in the State and Centre.

Educated girls have lot of aspirations like to marry late, to own property, to participate in the decision making process within the family as well as outside the family and so on. They also have the desire to overcome the social and traditional barriers imposed on them not only by their family members but also by the society at large. They wish to overcome the dependence and promote social and occupational mobility.

Chinar tree has special cultural & religious significance among Kashmiris both Hindus and Muslims. It is a popular symbol of Kashmir heritage seen in various designs of arts & crafts, articles of house and *shikara* decoration, embroidery of shawls, papier-mâché, wood carving and *namda/ gabba* making. Several articles of handicrafts decorated with motifs of Chinar leaves are source of curiosity for the tourists and pilgrims who visit Jammu and Kashmir.

The scenario pertaining to the drainage system presented a dismal picture of the overall Srinagar city. The defective and deficient drainage disposal systems of the city, as observed, continued to figure a challenging task and financially a heavy and disturbing proposition for all the concerned agencies.

Although literacy levels are low, there has been progress in improving educational attainment for both sexes in India over the last several decades. In 1971, only 22 percent of women and 46 percent of men were literate (Registrar General and Census Commissioner RGCC, 1977). By 1991, 39 percent of women and 64 percent men were literate (RGCC, 1993). This shows that there has been an increase in the proportion of women literates in just 20 years. But the condition is still far from satisfactory. There is a wide disparity in the education of boys and girls in the state of J&K as gender gap in the literacy of males and females is wide. The rural-urban gap in terms of literacy is also there, but rural areas despite the lack of infrastructure were not lagging much behind.

Like every society, the society of Ladakh is also undergoing change from joint to nuclear, reason for this structural change being the mutual conflicts among the members of families, job opportunities and education. With the spread of education, sons of farmers do not like to work as a farmer rather they chose to have proper education and jobs. For education and job opportunities they migrate to the town and settle there in and around town.

To study the Indian architecture it begins from the Indus period, so culture is an important part of our understanding of the times. As culture changed so did our understanding of the visual imagination changed. From early times, Kashmir which was the part of ancient Indian temples, had glorified the art and artistic nature of that era. Which are shown by these ancient monuments. These are categories in the Indian style of art and architecture, like Negara & Dravidian style. The architectural style of these monuments is very much similar to ancient Kashmir architecture of monuments.
In spite of all the efforts, societal attitude towards the disabled children have not undergone any radical change. Ignorance about disability is widespread resulting in deep seated prejudice about disability. Negative attitude dominate, and disability is thought of as a taboo and a stigma. Disabled children are often a terrible shock to their parents whose pride and self esteem have a rude shock and they begin feeling inferior and built walls around them before they come to terms with the reality. Some curse the stars operative at the time of birth of the child, other attribute it to their 'sins' or bad 'karmas' in previous life. This is primarily due to the social construction of disability in our society. As such, these children because of

their lower worth are denied the rights existing for the 'normal'. They remain enshrined in the ideologies of segregation, labeled and categorized according to the medical definition of their disability.

In district Kishtwar it is analysed through the present study that with the start of construction of the Dul Hasti project, the local unemployed youth got an opportunity to work with the contractors as per their qualification and experience. But on the other end there are certain negative issues related to such projects like rehabilitation and employment, natural disasters, relocation and alienation etc.

It was observed that various factors were responsible for taking or leaving science education in today's world. It has been observed that the effect of traditionalism is still in our society and it has to some extent affected the science education among Kashmiri females. Another factor is economic factor responsible for taking or leaving science education. As we know our Kashmir is not so much economically developed so it acts as a hindrance for taking science education because science education is costly it needs more and more money. It also comes that students have less awareness about the scholarships provided in science stream.

A vast number of rituals are more prevalently practiced in rural areas of Jammu and Kashmir. The rituals of Jammu and Kashmir were inherited from the ancestors and are still existent in full sway in the valley of Kashmir. Rituals like *Gada-Batta* (rice and fish), *Kaw-Punim* (love with birds), *Khachi-Mavas* etc. have an ancient past and are symbolic of theological philosophy, which predates the advent of the Sanskrit Aryans into Kashmir. These rituals have a proto-Aryan origin and should not be ascribed to any aborigines in the ancient past of Kashmir. They have rich theological background and cannot be explained by simplistic explanations, based upon Nineteenth century methodologies of history.

Issues and Problems in the Sociology of Jammu & Kashmir